Letters of Strindberg
TO HARRIET BOSSE

Here are the letters of a tormented genius of the theatre to his third wife, a young Norwegian actress. The renowned dramatist August Strindberg and the newly acclaimed actress Harriet Bosse met in 1900 in Stockholm. Soon Strindberg was wooing her stormfully and in 1901 they were married. The following year their daughter was born. A few years later they separated, and in 1908, when the letters break off, Harriet Bosse married another. Included in this collection are nine letters from the young actress to the much older, established dramatist.

In these letters Strindberg unreservedly lays bare his heart, and what stands exposed can very well be the key to the enigmatic interplay of man and woman in many of his famous plays. It is not correct to apply broadly the label "misogynist" to a multi-faceted genius like Strindberg and hope thereby to describe him. Only with the help of revealing letters like these, can we begin to fathom the man behind some of the most challenging plays of the modern era.

ARVID PAULSON

To date Arvid Paulson has translated into English more than a score of Strindberg's works as well as plays by Ibsen, Bjornson, Moberg, and other Scandinavian authors. He has been an actor for many years and has appeared in about one hundred plays. His first genuine success as Nogo in *The Willow Tree* condemned him for a while to play Oriental roles. In 1925 he wrote the radio version for the world radio premiere of *Peer Gynt,* which he directed and in which he acted the title role. He has given many readings from Ibsen and Strindberg, and is a permanent member of the Strindberg Society in Stockholm.

After reading Arvid Paulson's translation of Strindberg's final play, *The Great Highway,* Harriet Bosse asked him to undertake the translation of Strindberg's letters to her, and Mr. Paulson made up a collection from three previously published volumes of Strindberg's correspondence.

Letters of Strindberg

TO HARRIET BOSSE

EDITED AND TRANSLATED BY
ARVID PAULSON

The Universal Library
GROSSET & DUNLAP
NEW YORK

COPYRIGHT, 1959, BY ARVID PAULSON

ALL RIGHTS RESERVED UNDER
INTERNATIONAL AND PAN-AMERICAN CONVENTIONS

LIBRARY OF CONGRESS CATALOG CARD NUMBER: 59-10864

BY ARRANGEMENT WITH ARVID PAULSON

PRINTED IN THE UNITED STATES OF AMERICA

Introduction

During his turbulent life August Strindberg was married three times. His first wife was the fiery, vivacious Siri von Essen. After thirteen years of marriage they were divorced in 1891. The last years of their union were marked by frequent and often violent dissensions and tempestuous quarrels. He next married the young Austrian journalist Frida Uhl (1893). They separated soon after (1894) and were formally divorced in 1897.

Not long after he was married to Frida Uhl came his grave mental crisis which during the next three years threatened to break out into insanity and which reached its culmination in 1897. During this period his literary work came to a standstill and he began instead to pursue fanatically a variety of scientific experiments and studies through which he imagined that he would overthrow many existing scientific theories and attain world fame. He engaged in alchemic experiments and believed firmly he had solved the riddle of making gold. He suffered from hallucinations, delusions of grandeur and fantastic notions and considered himself a greater scientist than author and dramatist, despite the fact that three of his dramas (*Miss Julie, Creditors* and *The Father*) had at that time been sensational successes at Théâtre Libre and Théâtre de l'Oeuvre in Paris and that the French newspapers and periodicals were filled with articles and items about him, his personality and his literary achievements, as well as translations of some of his works.

He lived an ascetic life and suffered painfully from poverty. His hands frequently bled from raw sores that had been inflicted during one of his experiments. He suffered besides from chronic psoriasis, and for a time he lay desperately ill in the St. Louis Hospital in Paris. There he found solace and consolation through the ministrations of the mother superior: she filled the need of his Oedipus complex, which had remained with him from childhood. He was finally aided by Frida Uhl's family, by friends in France and in other countries, and chiefly by a benefactor in Sweden, the distinguished publisher and theosophist Torsten Hedlund. He went to Ystad in southern Sweden to consult his friend Dr. Anders Eliasson, an alienist. From time to time he visited Dr. Eliasson for treatment but would restlessly go from there to Paris, to Dieppe, to Dornach in Austria (where

v

Frida Uhl's family lived) and to the old university city of Lund in southern Sweden. At last he seemed to have recovered his equilibrium and to have found a semblance of peace of mind. He settled down in Lund at Christmas time 1896 and remained there, except for a half year or so in Paris, until the early part of the summer of 1899. He then returned to his native Stockholm. He lived there until his death on May 14, 1912.

In Stockholm he met Harriet Bosse. They were married on May 1, 1901, and on March 25 the following year their daughter Anne-Marie was born.

After his Inferno crisis Strindberg gradually reverted to his old self; but even after his mental and spiritual cleansing he was a recalcitrant. His old revolutionary spirit flared up at intervals despite his good intentions and his desire to be at peace with the world. He felt he had to speak out whenever a principle or what he considered the truth was at stake. If he did not, his conscience would rebel, his mental balance be upset. But when his anger was aroused, it was now more out of righteous indignation than out of vindictiveness. His old arrogance gave way to more tempered, charitable feelings, even to humility.

Strindberg was at his best as a playwright of moods rather than ideas. Perhaps the very reason for his greatness was his remarkable, intimate knowledge of every phase of human behavior, of human feelings, thoughts and desires that he had gained through bitter personal experience from earliest childhood. His growth as a dramatist can be ascribed to his constantly changing moods, his sensitive imagination, that gave birth to new impulses and ideas. A searcher throughout his life, he found inspiration in nature with its many wonders. He studied life with a microscopic mind, the writings of the ages, ancient as well as modern. He was an indefatigable student of every subject known to man, an accomplished linguist and musician. As he went along on "the great highway" of life he discarded ideas of the past for new ones, changing the form of his dramas and the treatment of his ideas, reaching into realms of the mind hitherto untouched by dramatists. That is why he will survive long after many of his day and other days, who have been crowned with the laurel wreath of glory, have been forgotten or have fallen by the wayside.

When Georg Brandes celebrated his twenty-fifth anniversary as an author he was fêted by literary figures, university students and representative men and women from many walks of life at a banquet in Copenhagen. Strindberg sent him a laurel wreath. Attached to it were these verses:

INTRODUCTION

> You—who have helped so many to win their laurels—
> received but thorns . . .
> Accept from a poet's hand now the wreath you bestowed
> on the poet.

It may truly be said that what Strindberg wrote to Brandes on that occasion, might be said about Strindberg himself with even greater claim, for all through life he bore a cross and his path was one of thorns.

Strindberg has been labelled a misogynist by many of his biographers. I cannot subscribe to this evaluation; and in her commentaries to these revealing letters of August Strindberg, Harriet Bosse likewise refutes this presumption. That label has been given him by critics who fail to realize that in most of his plays Strindberg delineated his characters objectively and logically, making both the husband and the wife share the blame for their inability to live together harmoniously. This is perhaps especially evident in one of his most devastating marital tragedies, *The Dance of Death*. Both Edgar and Alice suffer from grievous faults and are a constant source of irritation and outrage to each other. They therefore mutually bring about the horror that besets their conjugal union. Furthermore, Strindberg wrote about life as he saw it and as he had experienced it; and his experiences had been largely on the seamy side. It is true that his characters were not everyday types: they are often endowed with particular peculiarities and abnormalities, yet not so abnormal and rare that they are not to be found in our society, both of a past era and of today. Our divorce courts and our newspapers bear witness to that. The monotonous chores and tasks of everyday life, the succession of national conflicts and wars and the threat of impending ones are contributing causes for much of the contradictory behavior and the aberrant, neurotic confusion in the minds of many in our world today.

The Father, Comrades, Creditors, The Last Warning, Playing with Fire and *The Bond* (*The Link*) were written at a time when Strindberg's enmity to women's participation in politics, business and professional life (except as teachers, nurses and midwives!) was at its height. He felt passionately, almost hysterically, that woman's place was in the home, as wife and mother. It was also at that time that he began to show definite signs of serious mental depression and illness. The last years of his marriage to Siri von Essen were particularly stormy ones. He gave constant proof of his persecution complex, became suspicious of his wife, relatives, friends and servants. Small wonder then that he unleashed his fury through the characters in his plays. Yet throughout his life he sought a woman he could worship in his own way: as wife and mother. If Strindberg was a womanhater, it might be said with as much justification that he hated his own native land, for he often made acrid, venomous remarks both about Sweden, its capital and conditions there. Yet he proved both by deed and in his writings how much he really loved the country and city of his birth. And more revealing of his love for woman than anything else are these provocative letters to his third (and last) wife, the Norwegian-born Harriet Bosse, who became one of the great actresses of her time and who served as his inspiration during one of the most productive and important periods in his life. Some of these letters are gentle and lovely, some harsh and vindictive—still there is a touch of poetry and beauty about most of them.

When Harriet Bosse—after reading my translation of the great dramatist's final play, *The Great Highway*—asked me to translate the letters August Strindberg wrote to her, I read them and found them so interesting, so fascinating that I felt a compulsion to undertake the task. At Harriet Bosse's request Dr. Torsten Eklund, the eminent Strindberg authority and president of the Strindberg Society in Stockholm, first chose 25 letters from the volume published in Sweden by Natur och Kultur in 1932. However, I found the letters in this volume to be of such importance that I included practically all of them in the present volume, together with most of the letters in *De Återfunna Breven* (The Recovered Letters), published by Albert Bonniers Förlag in Stockholm, 1955. This volume also includes one letter from August Strindberg to "his unborn child" and nine letters that Harriet Bosse wrote (in Norwegian) to Strindberg. These ten letters were first published in the *Communications* of the Strindberg Society (Nr. 19, April, 1956).

Students of Strindberg's dramaturgy will discover many references to his plays and to the characters in them in these letters. They will also find suggestions as to how Strindberg would like to have them acted; and they will throw light on the great Swedish dramatist's chameleonic moods and character, his strange psyche, his indomitable spirit and remarkable genius: one of the truly great minds of all times.

I wish to express my gratitude to Dr. Eklund and to my friend Professor Walter A. Berendsohn, internationally known Strindberg authority, for their generous interest and kind suggestions in connection with the publication of these letters in English.

ARVID PAULSON

New York, N. Y.

A Note on Harriet Bosse

Harriet Bosse was born in Oslo, Norway, on February 19, 1878, the daughter of Heinrich and Anne-Marie Bosse. Her mother was born in Denmark, her father, a publisher, was of German ancestry. After studying music in Stockholm and acting in Norway, she made her début at the Central (Fahlström) Theatre in Oslo as The Princess in *Once Upon a Time,* later playing one of the daughters in August Strindberg's *The Face of Death,* Juliet in *Romeo and Juliet* and Valborg in *Axel and Valborg.*

She then went to Paris to study acting for Maurice de Féraudy at the Conservatoire, and in 1899 she was engaged by the Royal Theatre in Stockholm, where she made her début as Loyse in Théodore de Banville's *Gringoire.* She was immediately acclaimed both by the public and the critics. This appearance was followed by appearances as Anna in Gustav Wied's *The First Violin,* Puck in *A Midsummer Night's Dream,* The Lady in Strindberg's *To Damascus* (Part I), Eleonora in his *Easter,* Hedvig in Ibsen's *The Wild Duck,* Clärchen in *Egmont* and Isotta in *A Venetian Comedy* by Per Hallström.

In 1905 she left the Royal Theatre to accept offers to appear as a guest star at various theatres in Scandinavia and Finland. In the latter country she had then already been seen as a guest artist in the rôle of Kersti in Strindberg's *The Crown Bride,* which had had its première in Helsinki in the fall of 1904. By this time she had become recognized as Sweden's foremost actress of Strindberg rôles. In the fall of 1906 she was engaged by Albert Ranft for his permanent company at the Swedish Theatre in Stockholm. There she acted such rôles as Elga in Hauptmann's play of the same name, Indra's Daughter in Strindberg's *A Dream Play,* Ann in Shaw's *Man and Superman* and many others. In 1911 she was re-engaged by the Royal Theatre and remained there until 1918, when she again left to appear as guest star at other theatres and in motion pictures for the next decade and a half.

In 1934 the Royal Theatre again invited her to return to its fold, and she remained there until 1943, acting Electra in von Hofmannsthal's adaptation of Sophocles' tragedy of that name—a dramatically overwhelming, horror-striking performance according to the critics—Viola in *Twelfth Night,* Halla in *Berg-Eyvind and His Wife,* Liza in *Pygmalion,* Marguerite Gauthier in *Camille,* Henriette in

Strindberg's *Crimes and Crimes*, the title rôle in Shaw's *Saint Joan* and Cleopatra in *Antony and Cleopatra*.

Her acting was characterized by an extraordinary ability to endow her stage characters with a powerful individuality, and her art has been compared to a delicately sensitive instrument; she possessed a perfect mastery of technique, whether acting in classical tragedy or modern comedy.

After her marriage to Strindberg had come to an end, she was married to the actor Gunnar Wingård (1908) and after their marriage had ended in divorce in 1911, she was wed to another actor, Edwin Adolphson (1927–32).

In 1916 King Gustav V awarded her the decoration Litteris et Artibus for her artistic achievements.

A. P.

In the autumn of 1899 I was engaged at the Royal Theatre in Stockholm after passing an examination and reading one of Hans Christian Andersen's fairy tales before Nils Personne, who was then the artistic head of the theatre. "If you can learn to speak like a human being," he told me, "you will be engaged by the Royal Theatre."

In order to straighten out the confusion of my double-tongued language, I journeyed to Mme. Bertha Tammelin, an expert and renowned instructor in speech and linguistics, who at that time lived in the skerries. After having smoothed and polished my speech and diction for a couple of months, she considered me sufficiently ready to enter the Swedish stage. I made my début as Loyse in Théodore de Banville's *Gringoire* in August, 1899, and appeared the same autumn as an ingénue in a play by Ernst Didring.

That year there was considerable discussion in stage circles as well as among theatre-goers about Strindberg. His historical drama *Gustav Vasa* had had its première in October, 1899, at the Swedish Theatre and had been a great success. I was present at the opening performance and recall how excitedly the entire audience followed the drama act by act.

From that day I began to occupy myself with the reading of Strindberg's works. I read him every free moment I had, commenced to wonder about him and his personality, and felt a deep sorrow for him when I learned about all he had gone through.

Then the Year 1900 arrived. New Year's Eve 1899 I spent

at Skansen together with my brother who was then a cadet in the Norwegian army. I remember that I spoke a good deal about Strindberg with him. I told him I had never met Strindberg—and then suddenly had the impulse to wish him, unseen, a happy New Year. We wound our way to Banérgatan, where Strindberg lived at that time. His apartment was situated on the ground floor. It was dark and silent there. No doubt he had already gone to bed. With our noses pressed against the window pane, we stood there—my brother and I— and then I waved a happy New Year to him through the closed window. . . .

The scene was the dress rehearsal of Strindberg's *Crimes and Crimes* in February, 1900. The play was about to have its première at the Royal Theatre in Stockholm. Before my coming to the Swedish capital I had known only one of Strindberg's plays, the one-act tragedy *The Face of Death*, in which I had appeared at Fahlström's Theatre in Kristiania [Oslo]. I had been quite inexperienced when I came to the Royal Theatre the preceding fall. I had only a brief apprenticeship in the theatre behind me: a year of study and training in Kristiania and a few months at the Conservatory in Paris. What little I had had the opportunity to see of theatre in Sweden—with the exception of Strindberg's *Gustav Vasa*— was not at all to my liking. In my youthful superiority I thought that the acting was stilted, declamatory and false. The plays that I had seen seemed to me commonplace and uninteresting and were mostly conventional French comedies or sentimental German plays.

But at the dress rehearsal of *Crimes and Crimes* I sat completely fascinated. Here I found all the newness and freshness, which I had been yearning for—here I felt an irrepressible, untamed, uncompromising force, reminding me of the Norwegian literature, which I had been familiar with from childhood, and from which I had derived inspiration all through my formative years. But the equal of such unique genius, such originality and brilliance in modern dramaturgy I had never before experienced—and as I sat there among the audience, comprised solely of actors, chills ran down my spine, and I trembled with admiration and awe.

The spring of 1900 brought with it much work and a good deal of success for me. I acted Puck in A *Midsummer-Night's Dream* and Anna in *The First Violin*. Because of my success in these two rôles, the management began to take me into consideration when leading parts were being assigned. At this very time preparations were being made for the presentation of Strindberg's *To Damascus,* Part I, in the late autumn of that year; but the powers that be were undecided to whom to entrust the rôle of The Lady. August Palme, who at this time saw a good deal of Strindberg, proposed that they try me; and in order to offer him a generous selection of leading ladies, he suggested to the playwright that he view a performance of A *Midsummer-Night's Dream,* in which three of the Theatre's foremost actresses appeared, as well as myself, poor soul, who had been a member of the company scarcely a year.

Curiously enough, I was selected, primarily—as Strindberg later told me in jest—"because I had such nice legs." I would, of course, have valued the honor infinitely more if it had been my talent that had been responsible for the verdict!

As yet I had not met Strindberg in person. But one day Palme came to me with a message from Strindberg that he would like me to call on him the following day at a certain time.

This was in the spring of 1900. I was frightfully nervous at the thought that in just a few hours I would be standing in the presence of the man whom I admired so much and had wondered so much about.

I had no specially nice dress to put on. My wardrobe was limited to a grayish walking suit, which I thought most ill-becoming to me. I appealed to my always kind and helpful sister Dagmar. She lent me one of her gowns, a black one, that seemed to make me look slender and interesting. While it was tucked in here and there with safety pins so that it would not fall off, my sister being taller and less delicately built than myself, this temporary adjustment did not show when my jacket was buttoned!

And then a young girl, her heart in her throat and pins in her dress, marched up Narvavägen and turned off into Banérgatan. Outside the door I stood still before pressing the bell. I had to regain my composure somewhat.

Strindberg himself opened the door with a sunny, radiant smile. He invited me into a room, in which a table—heaped with wine, flowers and fruits—was set. No one could radiate charm as Strindberg, when he felt like it, and I was completely under his spell. We sat at his beautifully arranged table and talked about everything between heaven and earth. He spoke very little about his writings. On the other hand, a thought suddenly came to his mind and he rose quickly from his chair and went over to a cabinet, from which he took several large sheets of paper, smeared with a shining, golden brown mixture. He asked if I knew what it was. My face expressed only ignorance and curiosity. He then told me it was gold, which he himself had made. Naturally, I could not swear that it was gold—but, of course, I took it for granted that it was, since he said it was! And he was visibly delighted when I agreed with him that it was. Whether Strindberg was right in his belief that he had synthetically produced gold is something that time will show. Yet I am certain of one thing; if he had showed me a dog and called it a cat, I would—in blind adoration of his knowledge—have told him that, of course, it was a cat!

Toward the end of our conversation, Carl Larsson came

to pay Strindberg a visit. He screwed up his slanting eyes, lifted jestingly his finger in Strindberg's face and crowed: "What a rascal! The rest of us have to run after the lovely young creatures—but you—you entice them with fruits and flowers to come to you!"

And then I was asked where I intended to spend the summer; Strindberg himself was to spend it at Furusund.

When I was taking my leave, Strindberg asked if I would permit him to take a feather I had in my hat—he would like to keep it as a remembrance, place a steel pen in the quill and use it to write his plays with. I gave him the feather and obtained another, a similar one, for my hat. This one, also, was put to use by Strindberg as a quill while working on his dramas during our time together. The original one is now owned by our daughter Anne-Marie Wyller. The other pen is in the Strindberg Room at the Museum of the North in Stockholm.

After this visit I heard nothing from Strindberg until after the première of *To Damascus I* on November 19, 1900. Then came this letter, and with it a bouquet of red roses:

19 November, 1900.

Miss Harriet Bosse,

As I am not coming to the theatre tonight I wish to thank you now for what I saw at the dress rehearsal. It was sublime and beautiful (*To Damascus*), although I had imagined the character a trifle brighter, with little touches of roguishness and a little more expansion.

A touch of Puck!—That was my first word to you—and will be my last!

A smile in the midst of misery suggests the existence of a hope; and the situation does not appear to be hopeless, does it?

And now: Good fortune on the path of thorns and stones—for such is the road! I am merely placing a few flowers on it!

August Strindberg

Some weeks later came still another letter.

5 December, 1900.

Miss Harriet Bosse,
In view of our Damascus journey coming to a close today, I ordered some roses—with thorns, of course—as I believe no others are to be found! And I am sending them with this grateful thought: You will be our new century's actress! You have let us hear a new voice—wherever it came from! . . .
And give me the hope that I may hear you again—this spring—in *Easter*, as I believe you have promised me!

August Strindberg

   The year 1900 had passed, and the spring season 1901 was about to begin. Strindberg kept sending me books by the authors in whom he was interested at that time. I learned to know the contemporary literature, for the books he sent me were in the language, in which they were written. As I was somewhat behind in my education (as a child I had continuously travelled between Stockholm and Kristiania, and for that reason attended many different schools, with frequent interruptions of my studies) I could read neither German, French nor English without difficulty. I now began to study these languages seriously, determined to read the books Strindberg dispatched to me.

I made up a list of the subjects, on which I thought I was most uninformed. And then I proceeded to instruct myself several hours each day. I also started taking piano lessons again, in case I should find that Strindberg liked music.

One day he sent me the manuscript of one of his plays to read. It was *The Dance of Death,* Part I. It frightened me; and I will recall that I also conveyed this feeling to him in a letter, as he had expressed a desire that I appear in the play.

TO HARRIET BOSSE

[*8 February, 1901.*]

Dear Miss Bosse,

Glad to have had the opportunity at last to talk to you about *Easter*, I now seem to have forgotten so much of what I had wanted to say to you. Too, I fear you might think I am trying to interfere with your development. But as you today, so graciously and beautifully, thanked me—who desired to express thanks to you—I shall first of all say a few words about Eleonora, and later about another matter.

A grievous disaster in the family has brought Eleonora on the verge of a mental breakdown—called an illness by some—whereby she has entered into contact (telepathic) not only with her relatives but with all mankind, and the lower forms of life as well. She suffers with all living things: in other words, she manifests Christ in Man. Thus she has an affinity with Balzac's Seraphita, Swedenborg's Nièce—whom I should like to suggest that you become acquainted with as an introduction to *Easter*, if I were not afraid—yes—that I might be presuming. Also I had intended to ask you to read Hannah Joël's *Beyond*, Fru Skram's *Hieronymus*, and—above all—Maeterlinck's *Le Trésor des Humbles*. But, as I mentioned, I was afraid you might not welcome suggestions!

However, as to the keynote of the rôle: seriousness and solemnity, of course. Yet Eleonora must be kind and tender and should prattle and crow with Benjamin in an engaging manner, as when a child plays at little mother. Never hard, or even severe, she makes believe that she is knowing, would-be wise. As for her faith, we are left in ignorance of that; still hers is a cheerful, childlike trust. . . .

In order to show that she has brought an angel of peace with her, as her mother says, you must endow her with radiance and gentleness; and primarily, there must be no preaching or feeling of punishment, as among our pietists. And, note well, that when Benjamin asks whether she is a pietist, and she answers yes, she does so merely to cut short an inquisitive or indiscreet question; it is not a confession. Our pietists can not smile—but Eleonora can, because she believes in a beneficent God who will forgive, even though he occasionally

frightens children. You know—and this may sound curious—
I think I would like to ask for a touch of Puck, a little roguishness! Sad, by all means, but not severe!

I was indiscreet enough today to dissuade you from the tour. I cannot definitely tell you my motive, but I knew that they, who wish you well above all others, your sister and your brother-in-law, had advised you against it. No doubt this has had its influence on me!

And then also: I ask you to read the enclosed play and to determine whether you can fall in love with your rôle in it. The play has been submitted to the Opera, but note: it has not yet been accepted.

It is an attempt on my part to penetrate into Maeterlinck's wonderful realm of beauty, omitting analyses, questions and viewpoints, seeking only beauty in depiction and mood. That I have merely reached the portals, I am aware. I must first burn the refuse in my soul in order to be worthy of being admitted.

I beg you to read the parenthetical directions and to play the melodies—the primitive airs of Swedish folk music. Kersti is not incurably wicked, therefore you need have no fear of the contact.

Finally I beg of you not to confide this matter to others than your most trusted friends outside the theatre. You know from the above whom I mean. . . .

Another time, in the near future, I shall look forward to hearing what impression you have gained from *La Princesse Maleine*; and when you have read *The Crown Bride* I shall present to you the splendid, lovely girl Judith in *The Dance of Death*.

August Strindberg

Stockholm, 8 February, 1901.

Dear Miss Bosse,

The latest piece of intelligence from Chamberlain Burén —through Tor Aulin who is to write the music—reads as follows: "The Chamberlain will read *The Crown Bride* again."

—The first message was worded: "Yes, but we must have the assistance of The [Royal] Dramatic Theatre."

However, and as the decision may come momentarily, I beg you to give me a speedy answer as to whether I can count on you as Kersti—in order that I may promptly secure the rôle for you.

You, only you, possess the primitive essence of tragedy that is required—and I have been told you can sing, too, which is an added advantage.

But, dear Miss Bosse, do not reject my offer prematurely; let me conquer your apprehensions, and listen to me before you give your refusal.

If, by chance, the play is not accepted by the Opera, it will undoubtedly be produced by the Royal Theatre. I have already spoken with Personne—and then we would be closer to the rôle than before.

It is not impatience on my part that prompts this letter; it is the fear of losing you for the rôle, which might already have been promised to someone else.

August Strindberg

31 Banérgatan, Stockholm.
13 February, 1901.

P.S. Written on the assumption that you received the manuscript of *The Crown Bride* together with a letter last Friday. I am still uncertain that you did.

Stockholm, 16 February, 1901.

Dear Miss Bosse,

I continue to call you *dear*, because you were dear enough last Friday to ask God for his blessing on me . . . the first time in years anybody did that!—I don't know whether you believe in a good God, but He took you at your word and heard you! Can you believe it—I was sick and in darkness . . . and then came light—with good resolutions and peacefulness! That is why I kissed the little hand that had blessed me! May you understand now! And that is why I wept! It was not yesterday that I wept last! May you understand that, too!

Of course, you may keep *The Dance of Death!* I am awaiting your opinion with patience, and I pray that you will tell me afterward exactly what you think of the play.

One thing more, while I am writing to you. You say that you cannot act what you have not experienced! You can't really mean that, can you? You have not experienced Puck's roguish tricks, or the doubtful victories of *The First Violin,* have you? And yet you have acted them most successfully. Nor have you lived through the Lady's horrible Inferno journey with the Stranger (who now progresses with firm steps toward the cloister). And despite this you were chosen as the Pre-eminent, the New Century's Actress. Reconsider therefore your theory a little—and, if necessary, discard it!

Yours
August Strindberg

Dear Miss Bosse,

Would you like to attend a rehearsal performance at Miss Svensson's School of the Theatre? Then you will see, among others, Miss Sterner, who will not be likely to frighten you. You will also meet Richard Bergh and his wife there.

The school is at North Blasieholm Harbor (near Nybroviken, behind the Swedish Theatre) no. 5, four flights up.

Today the sun is shining and you are being given praise! It makes me happy—very happy!

Do not forget, please, to have the corrections in *Easter* inserted in the prompter's and the director's copies, referring to me (the author).

Faint rumors from the Opera concerning *The Crown Bride* have reached me. It should therefore be arranged that I hear you sing before long. One lone, simple folk song will suffice!

You know, I ponder and ponder how I shall be able to get you away from the minor rôles—but I have such a dread of appearing as liberator because I have always been a failure in that rôle.

Instead, let me say to you: Have patience! The small rôles teach you nothing, but they are purgatories that have to be suffered. If you pass through them, then you will have been set free!

Yours
August Strindberg

Will you give me your reply by telephone: Östermalm 29.46, if you can come this evening!
Stockholm, 22 February, 1901.

🙢 Through Palme Strindberg had submitted an inquiry whether I would be interested in playing Eleonora in *Easter*. Of course I was interested. I merely had qualms about the demanding rôle. I had already realized that the Lady in *To Damascus* exceeded my capacity and that I had only been partly successful in my interpretation of this rôle. But perhaps Strindberg, having in mind my imperfection, had written the rôle of Eleonora with so much simplicity that I could manage it. With this hope I set about to read the manuscript—and lost my courage completely. For if the Lady in *To Damascus* was a difficult task for a beginner, Eleonora in *Easter* was still more demanding. It required giving an intensive image of Eleonora's subtle nature with simple means and skillful technique.

I wrote so to him and received the following answer:

[*25 February, 1901.*]

Miss Harriet Bosse,
You must still have a little patience with me and my correspondence, which ultimately has in view our great common interest: Eleonora. Toward this end the books I am sending you, also have their purpose. You suggest that the character is so sensitive that it scarcely can stand being touched. And for that reason I will not analyze it or take it apart at the seams, nor philosophize over it. But, on the other hand, I would not like you to follow the traditional method of interpreting a deranged person. I feel certain you would not do

that, for you seem to be born with all the fresh ideas of the new century.

I noticed, too, after you had read Hannah Joël and Maeterlinck, that you had discovered a certain relationship, an affinity of soul, a way of seeing the world and the things therein—thus I content myself by suggesting those things that cannot be articulated.

Yesterday I sent you Kipling—exclusively because of the last story, "In the Land of Dreams."

In connection with that: Eleonora's double life in her dreams—in which she makes contact with far-away relatives. . . .

As I have mentioned to you: Do not study the books, but glance through them, and you will be helped by the hints that are given in them.

Why did I send you the bizarre *Le Prince de Byzance?* That is a very long story that would begin with Eleonora's close kin, Balzac's Seraphita-Seraphitus—the angel, for whom no earthly love exists because he-she is *l'époux et l'épouse de l'humanité*. A symbol of the highest, most perfect type of humanity, which has figured lately in the contemporary literature; and which by some is thought to be coming to earth to live. Ask no explanation now, but keep the word in your memory. One day, when this particular type of relationship falls within the sphere of your own experience, the word may cast some light on the matter.

One detail while I remember it! On page 15 in *Easter* there is a retort so cruel that I feel it as a wrong to Eleonora to use it. May I trouble you to change the terrible word "eat off" to "live off"?

And let them—together with the previous corrections—be inserted in the prompter's and the stage director's copies "at the request of the author."

[27 *February, 1901.*]

Miss Harriet Bosse,
  I have much to confide to you and much to ask you, but I have a feeling that my familiarity wounds you and my good will intrudes upon you. . . .
  However, rumors are now circulating that a reply may come from the Opera concerning *The Crown Bride* at any moment, and before it does it is necessary that I should have heard you sing, if only one single tune, so that I can say that I have heard you.
  It is, of course, improper for me to ask you to come to see me, and I have not the courage to do so. But if I should tell you that that troublesome table is, to be sure, set at two o'clock but will be cleared at two thirty, then you could feel free to honor me, as before, with a visit.
  If this piece of information should also seem tactless, please forgive me. I see no other way out for the moment.
  Enclosed is a letter from Germany that concerns you intimately.

August Strindberg

P.S. If you would care to telephone me—I am afraid this, too, is a tactless suggestion—then my number is: Östermalm 29.46.

[1 *March, 1901.*]

Dear Miss Bosse,
  Come and give me your impression of *To Damascus*, Part III, before it is watered down by something else.
  I place so much confidence in your judgment just because you acted the rôle of the Lady, you know.

Yours

August Strindberg

1 March, 1901.
Ö.: 29.46.

[11 *March, 1901.*]

Beloved Friend,
  Will you eat a simple dinner with me today, since the sun is not visible?

Should the sun appear, we can go to Hasselbacken for coffee. . . .
Enclosed is another telegram!
Did you sleep well?
Telephone your answer: Ö.: 29.46.

Your
August

Stockholm, 11 March, 1901.

Asked to pay him a visit in connection with the rôle of Eleonora, I went to see Strindberg, determined to ask him to give the part to a more accomplished actress.

This time also, the table was set and decorated with flowers and fruit. Strindberg was as usual amiable and kind. He begged me not to have any anxiety over Eleonora's rôle—I was bound to overcome any difficulties. He told me how hard and severe life had been to him—how he longed for a ray of light: a woman who could reconcile him to humanity and her sex. Then he placed his hands on my shoulders, looked at me long and ardently, and asked: "Would you like to have a little child with me, Miss Bosse?" I made a curtsey and answered, as though hypnotized: "Yes, thank you!"—and we were engaged.

After my engagement to Strindberg, I began to reflect on what had happened. I felt my responsibility tremendously. How could I give this man anything of worth? How could I, poor little creature, reconcile him to humanity and woman? What pleasure could he find in an exchange of thoughts with me, who knew so little about anything? I was frightened by the thought of the imminent marriage, but found myself incapable of confiding my thoughts on our union to him. It was not before the end of our engagement period that I took courage and wrote to him of my doubts. His letters of April 28 and May 1 came in answer to mine.

Strindberg's letter to me immediately following our engage--

ment is published here. I do not feel justified in disturbing its contents with any commentary.

29 March, 1901.

Beloved!
(Formerly "Dear Miss Bosse")
   Before you go to sleep tonight, I should like you to receive the blessing of the man you helped last Sunday!
   That little heart—your good heart—prevailed, as you see! May it ever prevail over. . . . . .

Your August

TO HARRIET!
(Written with the eagle pen)

Fear not the eagle, pure white dove!
Never—oh beloved!—will he rend you. . . .
Should you tire of your life on earth,
He will take you on his mighty wings,
Lift you high above the clouds!
Dove of mine so pure, the eagle is your friend. . . .
He protects you from the gray-winged hawk.
Guard him—and protect him from your arrows!

August

5 April, 1901

Palm Sunday, 1901.

Beloved,
   This morning I awoke with the feeling that last evening was the most delightful I had spent in our time—our . . . ever since my old timepiece went to its eternal rest in my tool box.
   There is an atmosphere of purity in your, Inez's and little Alf's home, which invigorates and refreshes me, makes me happier and full of hope!
   Purified through suffering, perhaps. . . . And you ask me to believe in you!—I believe so strongly in you, now that I have tested you; I know that you by nature have feelings that

I have striven to acquire—that you adore what I have dreamed of as a youth; that your spirit is pure as a child's—that you abhor what I deep down in my soul despise.

When the flower test is made in *Swanwhite*, the prince is rewarded with Swanwhite's love because his desires are pure—"and therefore stronger"! Anything else is mere weakness! Now I understand why the protagonist in *Inferno* had to capture the white banner before being permitted to hear the wedding march!

To me you are Swanwhite—and last evening, when I rested my world-globe head beneath what I like to call your celestial little globe, then I sensed that the universe had become harmonious—then I felt that my earth-spirit breathed something of the heavens from your unearthly spirit!

I had to write this—I could not speak it. Remember it—for it is true and real, more real than reality—yes, even more so than experience and the memorable events of life!

Your Gusten

Wednesday of Easter Week, 1901.

Beloved,
............You have suffered for thirty days for my sake, on the road to Damascus, suffered my agony; and now you shall suffer my *Easter*—you, my little Easter lamb!—When shall you derive some joy from me, through me?

I embrace you, I kiss your eyes and thank God for sending you, little dove, with a branch of olive, and not with a birch rod.

The deluge is over, the old swallowed up, and the earth will be greening once more!

Peace be with you, my beloved!

Your Gusten

Maundy Thursday, 1901.

Beloved,
What happened yesterday? If anything did happen!—But I have suffered through a whole passion play, staged in order

that we might be freed somewhat of our own love, and to the end that you—detached and with a purer love for your task (*Easter*)—might give humanity the poetry of suffering. The suffering for others, which is the deepest love of all!

Forget me therefore today! Follow your own supreme intuition, and you will not go wrong!

Remember only that I am with you in spirit, from my home—with good will and solicitude, and thus shall sustain you!

If you today can reconcile mankind to the thought that there is a God—and you will do that if you are gentle and not severe in your speech—then you will have performed a great service, greater than a work of art, no matter what its greatness may be!

But you must not make people afraid of God—for then they will move away from Him, from you and from me!

The Lost Father is anxious to be presented to His children—and you have been given the honor to bring about the renewal of the acquaintance. . . . Do it nobly, gently and beautifully! And He will love you—love us!

Your Gusten

Easter [Sun-]*day*, 1901.

Beloved,

Last night I felt as if God was angry with me and as if everybody hated me. And I wreaked my anger on all and everything.

Then I read your lovely letter, in which you thanked me for giving you light!

Can I, like Eleonora—herself so unhappy—provide happiness for others? Can my sufferings be transformed into joy for others? If so, then I must continue to suffer. . . .

I am thinking of the dark, ghastly electricity machine that reclines down in the cellar on Grev Magnigatan. It lies somber in the darkness, grinding out light for the entire block. . . .

What happened last evening I today realize was my fault. Last night I fell—downward, downward, pulling you down with me.

During the evening my ill-nature drew to me only the malicious and mean!
That was all!
Therefore: again upward! Will you?

Your Gusten

Easter Monday, 1901.
[8 April.]

Beloved,

As I am resuming negotiations with Personne concerning *The Crown Bride*, I must have your definite answer as to whether you will accept the rôle or not. For I am requesting that the rôle be given to you—have already done so!—and if you refuse it—well, then you have humiliated me, and you wouldn't want to do that, because "it would be a pity"!

If you will not accept my rôles, you refuse Swanwhite also. Do you then wish to see another actress take the place you occupy in my soul and become the Swanwhite who is [none other than] you? Is that your wish?

The consequences! Herr G. af G. has mentioned that he is writing a part for you; Herr Nycander has already written one for you; Herr P. S. will soon follow and Herr Tor H-g as well!

You should not refuse their rôles; yet these gentlemen—who themselves coach their actresses—will then enter into a spiritual relationship with you . . . while I remain an outsider.

How in that event will the life in common that we had dreamed of—in spirituality and truth—turn out? It will not materialize! And what will remain for us? Marriage—in which I am the steward who looks after your table, while all the others cater to your soul!

This morning I strolled along Narvavägen and glanced up at the little window of your room. I broke into tears—tears of longing and of sorrow—as of something lost, lost forever! What gave me that idea?

Why do you want to break away from me? And why do you

prefer any other soul to mine? Have I brought disgrace to you and your art?

Have the Lady in *To Damascus* and Eleonora degraded you? Will Kersti and Swanwhite do so?

You, who are young, were to grow with the new century and turn your back on the past. But this you are not doing—on the contrary you love the old, which was new and young twenty years ago!

Will you now give me a forthright, irrevocable answer about the rôle in *The Crown Bride*?

Your
August

Beloved,
Good morning! I wish I could see your little childlike mouth as you enter your apartment!
Brother Axel is now being sought for this evening!

Your
Gusten Strix

Stockholm, 11 April, 1901.

Beloved little Bosse,
Good morning to a new day!
In order to provide a slight change for the clergy, will you not step into No. 1 B on Jungfrugatan between nine and eleven and merely ask how the rector plans to communicate his answer to me regarding the forthcoming marriage banns: whether I must go there every day to inquire, or whether he will write or telephone.

With this, please note:
Forgive me, friend, for disturbing your enjoyment yesterday, but there are certain Forces over which I have no command.

As long as I stay peacefully at home, I have calmness; the moment I go out and mingle with people, the Inferno begins. That is why I long for a home of my own!

Your
Strix

31 Banérgatan, 12 April, 1901.

Beloved,
Good morning after a beautiful night! And thank you for the unforgettable evening with you—with you who make me forget all that is painful and bitter.

Your
Gusten

16 April, 1901.

16 April, 1901.

Beloved, beloved,
Spring is waiting for us, our short life is flitting. Our little bird's nest is built; the little souls that shall be ours, are waiting to be given form through our kisses—to be given tenderness and—the future.

What are we waiting for? Empty conventions of a past era! The respect of people, whom we disdain? My young, newborn, denominationless faith is stronger than that of the semi-faithless professional priest, is more powerful, more effective in invoking the blessing of the Lord God of Creation upon our union than any priest's.

My desire to make you happy is as earnest, as pure as that of any youth, and you can place reliance in me—for I believe in God! He punishes faithlessness and rewards uprightness!

Beloved, beloved! Hear my cry—the Eagle's cry: free, free, free! Come to me, dove of mine! I shall sit at the topmost crest of the mountain and keep watch! Today it is the serfs who make the laws; but the earls stand outside the law!

Well, let us stay outside the law under the immediate protection of the Eternal God! Follow me—now that all is ready!

Yours

[17 April, 1901.]

Beloved,
Your conscience is rebelling against the thought of being joined to a married man.

And nevertheless, the rector—as highest judge in this instance—has declared that I am not married, the Supreme Court in Vienna has officially issued the verdict that I am not wed, the Magistrates' Court here has not refuted it.

This is factual truth. Any other statement is loose talk. Do you know why Spring tarries, and what it is waiting for?

It is waiting to see two brave beings seal their love and their free faith with one resolve and one act.

A small cross shall be borne for a great faith, but I am convinced that a Simon of Cyrene shall in that very moment appear and remove the cross—[and with him] many others from Cyrene!

This is what I am dreaming now!

No church will open its portals for us. Very well, then let us walk alone, we lonely two, without seeking protection behind the opinion of spiritless friends. . . . We go of an evening in Spring, even if it should be snowing, into a church after the evensong is over; and there we kneel before the altar, vowing to be faithful to each other, exchange rings, and pray to God that He will bless our union. Then we walk to our home, we seat ourselves facing each other at our new table and we watch for what will happen in our minds—if we have been given peace—and outside us, for signs and warnings of God's displeasure. Should we find we have peace in our hearts, then we will be man and wife! If we find discord, then we must wait, sleeping with the sword of knighthood between us, watching for the renewed warnings of Providence.

But I am confident—I dream that the evening when we finally, by act and sacrifice, confirm our faith, then we shall have Spring, and on the morrow that follows, we shall be able to open the windows to let in the rays of the sun, and gentle, untroubled winds. . . .

This is my dream!

It is a smiling God who awaits us!

Therefore this breathless anticipation!

                        Your
                            Bridegroom

19 April, 1901.

Sublime, beloved Woman!

Hear me: If tomorrow the church is closed, I shall break it open, if you say the word, because it denied us admission to the God of blessings. We shall be wedded outside the little Gustav Adolf Church which is so dear to me because I visited it during the year I wrote *Gustav Adolf*—the champion of tolerance, for all faiths—and [even] for those who have no faith!

(But with witnesses! One must not disdain the judgment of one's fellowmen—and their support.) And after the marriage ceremony I shall affix this document to the door—without any din of hammer and nails, but merely with four tiny brass thumb tacks!

This having been done, we (leave our friends and) enter alone into our home, which will protect us. . . .

The document that accompanied this letter:

"I won't let go Your hand until You bless me."

This Christian Church having refused to open its portals and to unite our love in wedlock, we ourselves have exchanged rings, and vows of faithfulness, outside this chapel, beneath the great heavens and in the sight of the Almighty, and invoked God's blessing on our union as man and wife! Wanderer, go you and do likewise!—"My father and my mother have abandoned me, but The Lord receives me."

On the hillside outside the Gustav Adolf Church in Stockholm, 19 April, 1901, on Master Olof Day, at sunset.

August Strindberg   Harriet Bosse

21 April, 1901.

Beloved,

Yes—this is what I fear: that you will tire of sharing my painful, peculiar fate. . . .

As I sit before your Eleonora picture, I am aware of how much you have already suffered for my sake. . . . It is a female Christ image—the suffering for others!

But, beloved, do not try to change my fate, either from good will or love, for that would be dangerous. Through patience I have finally succeeded in bringing about a change for the better. Support me in these efforts and do not embitter me against Providence or mankind.

Stand by me until my fate is completed . . . I do not think it will be long now.

Never be angry with me . . . be compassionate! What you see is not temperament or disposition—it is my fate you witness. . . .

Help me bear it! I will never be able to overcome it. . . .
Yours

22 April, 1901.

My beloved little friend,

Must have a little talk with you before night falls.

I am pondering my bad luck (*Midsummer*). Well, it was not unprofitable. It brought me closer to those who were beginning to be irritated by my fame. I have a feeling that they like me better now that we have something in common: misfortune.

Not that they disliked me because I moralized—far from that! The time I *de*moralized, they grew irate, and justly so!

That I confessed my beliefs is not anything I ought to regret. I would be an ungrateful blackguard if I did not take advantage of an opportunity to tell the poor creatures from where I received help, and where they can find it.

It was unquestionably something else! But enough about that. . . .

I wonder what you are thinking about, having seen you so contemplative today. About your fate—which is now on the verge of changing?

What luck, dear friend, that you can rely on me today! That is something you would not have been able to do six years ago. For then I did not believe in anything.

Why are we faced with such hardships just at this time? In order to be cleansed by fire before our souls are wedded.

Perhaps some little soul is biding the time until we have swept and cleaned and put everything in order so that he can step down and share our home?

Perhaps our bodies must be burned to ashes before our souls can penetrate each other completely and become one.

Perhaps The Powers demand that we conceal ourselves in order that human glances may not touch what is meant to be concealed. . . .

Let us keep the faith that it is an expression of good will—then it will take on beauty and meaning!

Yours

Beloved,

A good morning after a good night, following a good day such as yesterday!

It is getting brighter? Well, we hope!

This messenger has also the practical task of bringing back the works of Péladan.

And I may see you, may I not—at twelve?—And press a kiss on your little baby mouth!

Your
Strix

28 April, 1901.
P.S. Today Schering is to confer about the Gustav Adolf
    drama.

[28 *April, 1901.*]

Beloved,

You ask if you can impart something good and beautiful to my life! And yet—what have you not already given me?

When you, my dearly beloved, my friend, stepped into my home three months ago, I was griefstricken, old and ugly—almost hardened and irreclaimable, lacking in hope.

And then you came!

What happened?

First you made me almost good!

Then you gave me back my youth!

And after that, you awakened in me a hope for a better life!

And you taught me that there is beauty in life—in moderation . . . and you taught me the beauty of poetic imagery—*Swanwhite!*

I was sad and grieving—you gave me happiness!
What, then, is it you fear?
You—young, beautiful, gifted—and what is much more: wholesome and good!—There is so much you can teach me! And you are rash enough to say that you would like to learn!
You have taught me to speak with purity, to speak beautiful words. You have taught me to think loftily and with high purpose. You have taught me to forgive an enemy. You have taught me to have reverence for the fates of others and not only my own.
Beloved! Who can tear us apart, if Providence refuses to separate us?
If it is the will of Providence—well, then we shall part as friends for life; and you will remain my immortal faraway Love, while I shall be your servant Ariel, watching over you from afar! I shall warm you with my love and my benevolent thoughts. . . . I shall protect you with my prayers!
Let us now wait until the sixth of May and see whether Providence desires to separate what He has joined together!
       Yours

[*30 April, 1901.*]
Beloved,
Good morning, and thanks for a glorious evening, always glorious with you.
The last day of April, the month of penance; tomorrow May, the month of flowers—our month—and Spring!
       Your
       Gusten

1 May, 1901.
Beloved,
I am just reading this: "I can fully imagine the little Lady's unrestrained joy, if the Stranger—despite her many misgivings—were to place her hands in his, serenely and silently, and set off with her toward—their goal!—And forget about the monastery!"
These were the words you wrote on March the fourth!

Has the Little Lady had cause to feel less happy, seeing what she has done for the Stranger in the way of beauty and high endeavor? The Stranger—whom she imbued with a loathing for "the beautiful pangs of conscience" and the Mosel intoxication . . . The Stranger, whom she gave back the true joy of life—whom she has taught to appreciate the Ninth Symphony, which is the acme of everything beautiful and peaceful, a lofty mood of solemnity, until it reaches the final chorus with its theme of joy. There the commonplace comes to the fore, and the Titan sings in popular vein, poking fun at the scatterbrained and the unthinking—who feel themselves oppressed by his mighty solemnity.

All this she has brought about. But she no longer rejoices . . . Has the pilgrimage toward her goal fatigued her, despite the fame and victories she has gained?

Is it possible that she has tired of her half-finished work of art, the vision of which was to give her joy and spiritual comfort from day to day, inspiring her to think well of herself and her mastery in creating beauty and goodness?

2 May, 1901.

Beloved,

In the midst of the prosaic, which nevertheless is so abundantly filled with poetry, a cry from the Eagle!

You wept last night, my dearest, because you are leaving your little cage and are being set free, free! Do you think that the lonely, gray little bird with the bloodbespattered breast, who flew to you last Christmas Eve and spread your Christmas table with joy, as you yourself expressed it—do you think that he could be a bird of prey?

Don't you think it will be he, who will be caged by you and become your prisoner?

And you have fears! You!

How must not the poor man tremble, then?

What is it you fear? The Little Lady showed no fears on March the fourth; for she knew that he loved her . . . And she still does . . . Her exultant joy when he took her hand, showed plainly that she loved him, too!

Thus: he loves her, and she loves him! What more do you desire? What is it that all the world and his wife are alarmed about? The past? But the past is over . . . like time, gone by—and no longer exists. . . .

Look to the future! Only the present and the future possess reality!

Let us embrace reality and speak of tomorrow! Tomorrow! . . .

My little sovereign, do you shrink from coming into your own home with your friend, your chief servitor, your own beloved—you, who have been so greatly endowed with the armor of youth, of beauty and talent?

Are you frightened?

🙦 These letters from Strindberg during our engagement period had, in one way or another, been lost. I presume that I had carelessly laid them here and there. After having been married a brief time, Strindberg came to me one day with the letters that he had collected and placed in chronological order. He asked me to hide them away. "There may come a day," he said, "when you will be glad to have them."

As a suitor Strindberg was extremely attentive. He sent flowers and presents; he thought about everything that could give me pleasure. He even forced himself to dine with me at Hôtel Rydberg, although he abhorred appearing in public places. But that dinner had an unhappy ending, for an unfortunate army officer, seated at an adjoining table, gave me a few glances—I was just beginning to be known as an actress. But the poor officer should never have done that! The hairs on Strindberg's upper lip stood on end, and with a snarl in the direction of the officer, he said to me: "Come! Let us go—I can't stand this!" This was our first and last visit to a public restaurant. We did, however, dine at Bellmansro and Djurgårdsbrunn, but invariably in a private room.

He enjoyed taking a drive in a victoria. Occasionally it went without mishap—but, oh, how many times the carriage was ordered, I looking forward with pleasure to the drive, ready to step into the victoria, when—from tightly closed lips—would come the words: "No—I can not . . . Let us go up again. . . ."

My memory of our engagement period is, with the exception of my own dread of how it would all end, only bright and beautiful.

There is no doubt that, during our engagement period, Strindberg was in a state of happiness and that this inspired him to write the fairy play *Swanwhite*.

We were married in May, 1901. Strindberg did not permit me to bring any of my possessions to the home he had furnished for me. I was to come merely as I was. Thus I abandoned everything I had in the room I had occupied for several years at the home of my sister, and made my entrance into the apartment that Strindberg had made ready for us at Karlavägen 40 (now no. 80).

Strindberg did not have what is commonly considered good taste as far as furniture is concerned. He had no eye for, or perhaps I should rather say did not bother about tendencies of style or period. I neither had the courage nor the desire to criticize his taste in surrounding himself with sofas of the 1880 period and with pedestals and aspidistra, dining-room furniture in ghastly imitation of German renaissance, and so forth. But gradually I came to realize that he saw, in his own way, something significant, even beauty and meaning, in such furniture. In Strindberg's study stood two sad looking cabinets of walnut of the 1880 period. One day he pointed out to me lines in the wood, which formed strange looking faces. And the images of old men carved in the buffet added in their peculiar way fuel to his imagination.

When he was writing *A Dream Play*, he bought a number of Oriental table cloths; and the design in a curtain might be instrumental in creating a mood for him. He loved the view he had over the expansive drill field (Gärdet), and he has utilized this scenically in some of his works from the period when he lived at Karlavägen. When he, for instance, speaks of the Castle in *A Dream Play*, it is the Horse Guard barrack with its cupola, visible in the distance from our home, beyond the drill field.

As to the coming into being of *A Dream Play*, another episode comes to my mind. Strindberg wrote the rôle of Indra's Daughter for me, and I created it at the original performance at the Swedish Theatre in Stockholm. That he made the part the daughter of an Eastern God came about through his indulging in fantasies about my Eastern origin. "You are from Java," he often used to say to me.

Where today stands a row of modern buildings, there were at that time—directly opposite our home—a potato field and an old barn. In the latter was stored theatrical scenery. The barn has been immortalized in *The Secret of the Tobacco Barn* (*Tales*). The Singer in this story lived in the house next door to us. The swarms of crows that used to invade the field can be remembered from the stanzas about the crows in the poem *Chrysaëtos* (*Trinity Night*). The greater part of *Play on Words and Art in Miniature* is written with motifs from our home, barring a few poems inspired by our summer stay at Furusund a year or so later.

My little drawing room Strindberg had furnished in mahogany—imitation empire. He had had the floor covered with a green carpet: it reminded him of a fragrant meadow. Then he had bought a flaming red cover for the chaise longue in this room. But it was quickly removed, as he found that it offended his eye. Nothing was permitted that was likely to lead one's thoughts to anything earthly and material. As may be remembered, this was during his spiritual crisis—he had turned his back on the world and was striving toward "the life beyond."

It was in these surroundings I now was trying to make myself feel at home. But I, for my part, was not even remotely finished with this world. I had only just begun to take a peek at it. How many times have I not sat gazing at the sun, gleaming over the drill field; it never brightened our rooms, as the windows faced toward the north. And so I wept and pulled down the shade in order to be spared seeing how beautiful the weather was outside.

One day Strindberg came into my room and told me, to my great delight, that we were to take a trip to Germany and Switzerland. We began to plan, ordered round trip tickets, packed our trunks, and looked forward with indescribable joy to the journey. The very morning we were to depart, and just as we were about to leave with our baggage, he gave forth a groan: "We are not going . . . The Powers do not wish us to. . . ."

It became my task to cancel the tickets and the hotel reservations. There was nothing to do but to stay at home and try to choke down the tears. . . .

In order to cheer me up, Strindberg arranged the dining-room table with fruits and Rhine wine, and we seated ourselves by the window, where we had a view of the drill field and the sun. He spoke of how much more beautiful it was to see the sun illuminate, light up, than to have it in the eyes; how much better it was to see people at a distance than to be plumb in their midst—and with this he gave me a Baedeker to read a trip in, as a means of avoiding all the troublesome actualities of a journey. But to me—who loved both the sun and people and traveling—this was scarcely a substitute! In any case, I tried to heed his warnings to me about life and people; he had nothing but my good at heart, was eager to protect me against the hardships he himself had endured—although he failed to take into consideration how impossible it was for me to transport myself from my twenty years to his fifty!

I grew impatient and nervous, when he—to comfort me for the disappointment of not taking the trip—brought me books to read in English, French and German. To make matters worse, I was to struggle with foreign languages! It was then I sobbed out my determination to travel alone to Hornbaek in Denmark, as long as he did not want to come with me. And so I did! I arrived there alone, and met there by chance the first day the distinguished opera singer Herold of the Royal Opera in Copenhagen. As I was convinced that Strindberg would not be long in following me to Hornbaek, I asked Herold to help me find a house I could rent for the summer. After wandering about for a while in Hornbaek—so delightful in those days—he took out a coin and said: "Wherever this coin falls when I throw it—there is where you are going to live . . ." Quite close by was an attractive little house, covered by ivy, and there was where the coin rolled. And it turned out that the house was for rent. . . .

That same day a letter came from Strindberg. When I left him in Stockholm, I was griefstricken and ready to die. But in Hornbaek, where I was now, it was so beautiful that I could not help but feel that life was worth living. . . .

Letter to Hornbaek, Denmark

27 June, 1901.

Dearest, beloved wife,

So many tears, so many tears, and so scorching that they burn out my eyes! And why? Mostly because I am plagued by the thought of all the sufferings I involuntarily have brought upon you . . . But at the height of my self-accusation I cry out: But I could not have acted differently! I could not. . . .

And still, when I come into the golden room, I see you— see you such as I found you that day—sitting there in agony, weeping . . . and then my heart nearly breaks from grief and pain. . . .

I thought I had learned to resist the pain of suffering—but this—this was more than I could bear. And last night—I thought I would suffocate from weeping . . . and in the darkness I fumbled for the little hand that made me feel so secure against the horrors of the night when I held it in mine. . . .

The feeling of my loss—the grief—the uncertainty—the pangs of conscience. . . .

I never step outside the door—but remain here in my hermitage. . . .

Yet not alone—for in here you are everywhere—in your regal beauty—with your gentleness—your innocent smile. . . . Was all this necessary in order to make me realize how deeply I love you?

No—for I knew it when I said to you: You now hold my life in your hand, Harriet! If you leave me, I shall die!

If you are leaving me . . . if you have left me—I do not know. . . .

Leaving me—having left me—without having reconciled me to humanity—and woman!

29 June.—Your telegram "I am living," a demon whispered in my ear to translate into: "I was dying while near you! Now that I am away from you, I can live!"

The same day.—After having wept in my retreat, which I have not been outside for three days, I received your letter.

Do I not love you?—Woe—who has whispered such thoughts to you? If you were here, you would see what kind of existence I lead without you! You would read how beautifully I have described our entrance into our home! "Flowers on the table—the flames of the lighted candles in the candelabra stand still in devotion—the flowers are silent in thought."

And now the lights are going out by themselves! It is growing dark in the dining-room—but still can be seen the sun-yellow, gilded shade of the brass lamp in your room—the pale-green room—green as a midsummer meadow. . . .

He is frightened by the darkness . . . She stretches forth her little hand, the soft, delicate, gentle hand—the little hand in the darkness! And she leads him toward the sunshade—toward the light in her pale-green room. . . .

And he thanks her who has reconciled him to mankind and woman. . . .

My dearest! Can you not feel at a distance—distance is something that does not exist for us—that I am living only in you, that I love you?

You are with me all the day long, and the incense of your being sweeps to me here through space. . . .

Are you not conscious of my longing?

Do not my tears give solace to you when you are in grief? I shall cry—cry like a child—in the belief that my tears will fall on your poor little heart!

What can be the meaning of this?—Yes—a trial . . . I hope merely that! The self-accusations lacerate me, but I cry in my hour of need: I could not do otherwise!

I *could* not go with you—yet I had no right to seek to prevent you when you finally left. . . .

I am sitting here guarding your home, pleading with God for patience to be able to witness the day when you—shall return to me.

I no longer see you in the flesh . . . I see only your soul, its beauty and goodness—which you were beginning to forswear. I hold your inner image so pure, so chaste, lest it be soiled by even a breath of evil! I keep before me only Eleonora's Christ head . . . Poor Eleonora, whose mission it was to help him share his suffering!

Beloved, if you should realize at last that we are united by the mighty, sacred bonds of love, then call on me! And then we can meet in Sassnitz! Only there!

Your Gusten

Strindberg came both to Elsinore and Hornbaek.

The little ivy-covered villa has since been memorialized in several of his poems: in *Chrysaëtos,* for instance. After spending a month in Denmark, his visit came to an end. It so happened that an unsuspecting photographer, who took a snapshot of me while bathing at the seashore, was rewarded by a blow on the head from Strindberg's walking stick. As a result of this incident, the newspaper *Politiken* in Copenhagen opened its columns to a discussion as to whether or not photographers should have the right to take pictures freely at the seashore. We fled this discussion and arrived in Berlin some time early in August, 1901. I was not allowed to remain in Berlin; instead I was taken to a *pension* at Grunewald, near which Strindberg's German translator Emil Schering had his home. I did not feel at home there in the slightest; as a matter of fact, I was taken ill. The sicker I became, the more brightly Strindberg's eyes shone—and then he told me that I undoubtedly had become pregnant. Strindberg was deeply in love with his children of previous marriages; but through fate they had all been taken from him. His home, wife and children he looked upon as life's greatest happiness . . . and now he was waiting joyfully for the arrival of my little Anne-Marie.

Our stay in Germany was not long. We returned after a brief period to Stockholm, where I was due to appear at the Royal Theatre. During the autumn season of 1901, Strindberg's *Charles XII* was to have its original presentation there, and I had been chosen to appear in the rôle of Emerentia Polhem. The première, however, was postponed (it occurred in February, 1902) because of my indisposition. Later in the season that year I acted the rôle, however.

During the time I was unable to appear on the stage, I recall that Strindberg tried to help me to pass the time pleasantly. He suggested that I ought to try sculpturing. I was convinced I possessed not the slightest talent in that direction; yet he encouraged me to attempt it. He bought a sculptor's cavalette for me, and clay—and all I had to do was to set to work. I was to model myself as Puck. Strindberg was my teacher. He corrected me and gave me encouragement. When the statuette was completed, he exhibited it with pride to

Richard Bergh who—no doubt out of courtesy—praised it. Strindberg had my work cast in bronze, in twelve impressions, which, as I recall it, he presented to friends and acquaintances.

While I was sitting in my room, toiling and plodding at my sculpturing, Strindberg put up his easel in his room. He painted a host of pictures, of which two were given to me. One of them—the only one with sunlight that Strindberg, to my knowledge, ever painted—is now in the National Museum. The other one, a dismal sunset among clouds and barren cliffs, with a few scrawny flowers in the foreground, is still in my possession. As Strindberg never signed the canvases he painted during this period, I have inscribed my name on the two he gave me, and the year in which they were painted, in order to preserve the date.

During this period, too, he produced a large painting—I believe the fifth one with the motif he was so fond of using. He called it the Wave—one lone, black, mighty ocean wave.

When Strindberg was about to commence work on a painting, and I asked what he intended to paint, he would answer: "I don't know. I have to wait until it is finished."

He seldom used a brush; he preferred to smear on the paint with a palette knife.

I have no particular recollection that Strindberg discussed the art of painting with me to any great extent. But in order that I would not be completely uninformed, he gave me reproductions of, among others, Corot and Millet, and presented me Laurin's *The History of Art*.

Strindberg had many friends among artists, particularly Richard Bergh, Karl Nordström and Eldh. He sat for paintings and busts they made of him, but he never was critical. Still I can remember that he once said to me: "Why must they always make me look so austere, ugly and frightening?"

Whenever I was not sculpturing, I had to devote myself to reading. To Strindberg I am indebted for my entire literary education. Among other authors, I read Balzac, Maeterlinck

(Strindberg was so fascinated by Maeterlinck that he amused himself by translating a chapter from *Le Trésor des Humbles*, dedicating the manuscript to me), Zola, Gorki, Emerson, Kipling and Kielland. With Björnson I was already acquainted —I was in love with his folk tales. As is well known, Strindberg was not enamored of Ibsen. His play construction he considered dry and dull—and besides, Ibsen was the champion of women! No author of the contemporary Swedish school elicited any special interest from him.

[After Strindberg and Harriet Bosse had returned from Berlin in August, 1901, the strain of living with her husband became too great for Harriet Bosse. On August 22 she left him, and on August 27 came a letter to her from Strindberg.]

[*About 27 August, 1901.*]
Say but one word—about your intentions—as soon as you yourself have made up your mind about them.

I cannot think of any means to induce you to return, as I do not know why you went away. But if you, for your part, are waiting for a word from me, then I need not say that your home is waiting for you, and just as clean as when you left; and that you can enter your yellow room, and your green one, whenever you please, without seeing a glimpse of me; that you can close your doors; that you can open them and call me whenever you so desire; that you need make no explanations; and that I shall be as little disagreeable to you as I can possibly be!

August Strindberg

A letter from Harriet Bosse to August Strindberg

Stockholm, 27 August, 1901.
Can't you understand why I went away? I left in order to save at least the final remnant of what remained of womanly modesty and self-respect.

The language you used to me that memorable day in Berlin

has been ringing in my ears. The accusations you then made have affected me so that even the most endearing words from you could neither remove their sting nor conceal their ugliness!

It was this feeling of shame that took hold of me these last few days with a force so compelling that I felt I would be the lowest among women if I, after what had happened, continued to live with you, and to endure it.

I kept accusing myself of being a coward—a coward for not leaving you that day in Berlin. But my excuse is that I was ill. . . .

And if I should come back to you again, then you would naturally feel still more contempt for me. And the next time you were angered over one thing or another, you would again —and then even more viciously—heap over me such words as I can't imagine any man could use, even to the foulest streetwalker—least of all to his wife.

No, Gusten, I will not be rendered unclean so blatantly, least of all now that I am expecting my beloved little child! It must be born in purity! . . .

You must know that I have not had it too easy these days— for you are, despite everything, the father of my child. But rather than to look forward to a horrible future, filled with falsehood, ignominy and pain for us both, I am leaving while I still have all the beautiful memories of what you have given me, in fresh remembrance.

Do you recall what I told you repeatedly: I shall do whatever you wish me to do—as long as you treat me with kindness!?

Harriet

[*28 August, 1901.*]
I stretched out my hand to you yesterday.—That generally signifies: Let all that was painful be forgotten; it carries the message: forgive and forget! But you did not accept it. May you never have to regret this!

How often during the nights . . . have I not taken your outstretched little hand and kissed it, even though it had clawed me—merely from mischievous, childish whim to claw!

I recall one night: I kissed your hand with a prayer that you would sleep well, and you reciprocated by kissing mine. And then you gave vent to a reflection . . . which I shall never forget . . . Do you remember what you said?

There are words that must be spoken despite one's disapproval of them, in spite of suffering from their sting. Such a word was the one you took so to heart when last we saw each other. But it was a stick of dynamite placed on the railroad track as a signal of warning before [the critical moment of] danger.

Do you recall what it was that set it off? You wanted to deprive my child of my name. I made the remark that if my child were given the name of B., it might hurt the child all through life, and that her comrades would some day get the idea that she was born out of wedlock.

But long before this you had played with the poison. When it became apparent that you were in a blessed condition, surprised at this, you uttered insulting words! You "could not grasp how it had happened!" Later you began to cast insinuations that the child was not mine, that it could not be mine, simply could not be like me—in a word, you played the rôle of poison mixer. And then go back to that other time, when we feared that you were with child, and your outburst that night at the inn at Hornbaek, when you gave thanks to God that you were not in that blessed state, and emphatically spoke of "virtuousness." Incredible!

Recall further the first weeks of our marriage. The day after we were wed, you declared that I was not a man. A week later you were eager to let the world know that you were not yet the wife of August Strindberg, and that your sisters considered you "unmarried."

Was that kind? And was it wise?

If the child is not mine, then it must be someone else's. But that was not what you meant to imply. You merely wished to poison me; and this you did unconsciously. To bring you back to your senses, I awakened you with a shock.

Are you awake now? And can you resolve not to play with crime and madness in future?

You write that you have not had a happy life. What do you think I have lived through? Having seen what I considered sacred treated as buffoonery, having seen the love between husband and wife after so short a time exposed to public view—I came to regret that I had ever taken anything seriously, was driven to believe everything in life to be colossal farce and fakery! I wellnigh lost my faith—in everything!—and came very near to falling back into malignity, decided to write farcical plays, colossal ones, farces about love, about motherlove, about world history, and about sacred things. I had thought of writing a parody on *Swanwhite* for Anna Hoffman—but when I came to the *Easter* girl I stopped.

You once asked God to give me His blessing for having written *Easter*. Did you speak honestly that time? If you did, how could you—eight days after our marriage—exalt Lindelin as your womanly ideal . . . and say that you could not be an artist without first being a harlot?

And you glorified adultery, threatened to take a lover, bragged that you could acquire one whenever you desired . . . It was in this manner you sought to give me back my faith in woman—and in humanity!

And now you ask: How can I, in spite of all this, still love you?

You see: Such is love! It suffers all—but it will not tolerate humiliation and debasement!

And at the very moment that our marriage was to be cleansed and ennobled through our child—you take leave of me!

Where do you desire to have your belongings sent? To Grev-Magnigatan or to Blasieholmen?

[August Strindberg]

[*About 29 August, 1901.*]

In this spook tale, which is called our marriage, I have sometimes suspected a crime. Will it surprise you that I momentarily have believed that you have been playing with me, and that you—like Emerentia Polhem—had sworn you would see me at your feet.

This suspicion I expressed later to Palme after the inexplicable scene at the dress rehearsal of *To Damascus*. I still believed, from your first visits in February, that you were toying with me, but that your feelings gradually would change and that you would become sincerely attached to me. I presume you know it to be true that there was wickedness in your eyes and that you never gave me a friendly glance. But I loved you and hoped unceasingly that I would finally meet with love in return.

When—following the wedding—I saw your spiritual decay; the forms your maliciousness took; how cynically you regarded what to me was holy; how you despised me; how melancholy and anguish took hold of you—then I thought you were tortured by a bad conscience, for it is in this manner it asserts itself.

That you had betrayed the secrets of the yellow room, that I could understand—and I forgave you, even though I was horrorstricken and wept inwardly.

When I saw your portrait hanging in the shop windows between two similar portraits of a certain actor, I trembled with dread. And when this actor was struck by a bullet in the chest, I felt as if a protecting Power stood watch over me and saved our holy union.

I once thought you loved me: when you returned from the visit to Inez in the skerries . . . then there was harmony—and it was then, I think, that our child was given its life.

In the evening you radiated a supernatural beauty at the dinner table and you gave vent to these words: "Oh, now I feel that I am a woman!" Our child has been conceived in love, after all, and not in hatred; in pain and not in pleasure! Therefore it is legitimate; and that is the difference between legitimate and illegitimate offspring! For where sensual pleasure is sought, there will be no children!

Your absolute distaste for seeing Richard Bergh again I have sought to explain, by guessing, in this manner: that the secrets of the yellow room had been confided to him last spring and that you now had a feeling of shame. It is possible that I have been mistaken. In which case he must have behaved indiscreetly toward you, and if so, you ought to have indicated this to me so that I could have broken off the friendship without explanation.

This—our marital relationship—is to me the most inexplicable thing I have ever experienced: the most beautiful and the ugliest. At times the beautiful stands forth by itself—and then I weep, weep myself to sleep that I may forget the ugly. And in such moments I take all the blame upon myself alone! When I then see you, melancholy, agonized—in May and June—in your green room, sorrowing over your lost youth, which I have "laid waste," then I accuse myself, then I cry out in pain because I have been wicked to you and wronged you . . . I kiss the sleeve of the garment from which you stretched out your little hand, and I plead with you to forgive me all the misery I have inflicted upon you!

When I have shed all my tears and the Angel of the Lord has consoled me, I can think a little more calmly . . . this is the way all young girls have grieved over their youth and through these portals of grief have entered into the domain of motherhood, where woman comes into the greatest joy of life, the only true joy—and which she divines instinctively beforehand . . . You have already sensed and experienced it!

But I—who was a partner in this grief—I am not permitted to share the happiness!

Is it my fate to give life to children, to be weighted down by worries and ingratitude, and then to have all the joy torn from me? Then do not say that it is I who flee from happiness!

When I once made a remark that our home was like a ghost home, you answered: "If you knew what took place in this house, you would die from horror."—What was it that happened here, of which you were aware but not I?

Suppose that our relationship is tainted by hate and suspicion—everything becomes soiled in the autumn—but the new Spring that the child is bringing us will destroy and place in the background our selfish love. Can we not put aside our personal illusions and be joined only in mutual interest as parents and friends, and meet in artistic endeavor, which is our common ground?

And have you given no thought to our child that cries out to be born in a home; that demands a father and a mother, tenderness, consideration, support, and later, an introduction to life?

A child, growing up without knowing its own father who is known to everyone else . . . And should you die, do you think I would be prepared to receive a child brought up to hate me?

What does all this matter to you?

What is to happen now? I don't know, but I long for an end of this—even if it be the very worst!

[*2 or 3 September, 1901.*]

My life, my thoughts, and my pen! I wished to lay all at your feet, for I loved you! But I had no desire to descend again into the ugly and the vile!

And we were settled in a home, a home given us by God, you said . . . And the pigeons built their nests under our cornice, and the swallows, too . . . And you thought our home more beautiful than any other. But then the gold in your ring of faithfulness turned black and you found it in turn dull and ugly . . . But the yellow room still had the clean fragrance of my true, strong, pure love—and then I was driven out by your hate . . . And behold, the yellow room became malodorous. It was your selfish hatred that gave out the stench—it was not I. . . .

How long do you think I can wander here among the dead? Not for long, for then I shall soon find myself in the grave—and I have nothing against that; yet I have duties to perform in life.

Tell me therefore whether I shall expect you or not . . . Every hour is an hour of pain, and I must get out of here if you are not coming back!

What is it you demand of me, what terms do you set up?

Yesterday I was on the point of breaking up our home, destroying all our memories—all . . . and—as I cannot travel —again putting up with other people's furniture in a furnished room!

Then I shall ask God that I may be given the grace to forget you, forget your name and that you ever existed—you, whom I once spoke of as my "first wife."

I have cherished a hope: your letter from Denmark, when you departed the previous time without leavetaking. I read from it: "Beloved! What is this? Our hearts, which have been welded together by a kiss of God. . . ."

And it ends—with this cry of distress: "Oh, my beloved friend!"—I have now wept outwardly until my eyes have paled and inwardly until my soul has been cleansed!

I have kissed your image and called out to you, and if you had been dead I would have sorrowed for you until you had risen from the grave!

For the last time: Come back to your yellow room! There alone you will find tenderness and care, and there alone shall our child see the light of day!

Come, whatever moment of the day you choose. Call upon Lovisa and she will accompany you past my door, which will not open until you give the word!

You need not reply to my last two letters! They constituted answers in themselves, and they contained no questions!

From Harriet Bosse came this letter to Strindberg.

3 September, 1901.

For some time now I have tested myself in order that I might at last give you a definite answer.—For the sake of us both it is best that I do not return. A continuation of life together with suspicion of every word, every act of mine, would be the end of me. And as for you, you would be plagued and excruciated by these fancies; and words—which you most certainly would regret afterwards—would again cross your lips.

Is it not better, then, that you carry on your life's mission, your *creative writing*, without me—by yourself alone? And that I continue the career I have begun—and which for me is the most important thing in my life, next to the little one I am expecting?

To work together was our goal. I think it is best accomplished this way, apart from each other. That way, we gain respect for each other; and the disagreeable qualities we have found in each other will be dissolved and wiped out by time and distance. You have given me so much that is beautiful, Gusten! I thank you for all that! It has been a joy for me to have been entrusted—act by act—with your work: a recognition I was proud to receive from you.

Our little child shall be gentle and good. I shall always speak well of you to it. Of course, it will bear the name of Strindberg.

If you feel that you can, it seems to me that you ought to remain in the apartment on Karlavägen. There you have truly a home that you should not give up.

I shall, for the present, live in a *pension;* and Lovisa will look after my belongings.

You must not think badly about me now. To make excuses is of no avail: you yourself must feel what is the truth, and what is not.

I have imprinted a kiss from your child on the letter!

Harriet

[*4 September, 1901.*]

To my child! (The unborn little one)

My child! Our child! . . . Our Midsummer child! Your parents walked about in their home waiting for something—and all waiting being long and frequently tedious, they imagined that they themselves were dull and tiresome.

They waited for something to arrive. They were not aware that it had come—in a quiet, fragrant room with yellow walls—yellow as gold and sun—beneath a canopy of white gauze. . . .

Then your Mother was gripped by a longing to see her Mother's native land—an intense longing that tore her with bleeding heart from home and hearth.

In the pale green wood of beech by the blue sea you were carried, child of North—and Southland. . . .

And your lovely Mother cradled you upon the blue waters

that sweep three kingdoms . . . and in the evenings, when the sun was about to set, then—then she sat in the garden, looking the sun in the face, that you might be given the sun to drink of.

Child of the sea and the sun, you slept your first slumber in a little red cottage of ivy, in a white room, where words of hate were not even whispered and where nothing impure was even thought. . . .

Then you made a dismal journey—a pilgrimage to the City of Sin [Berlin], where your father was to weep. . . .

And then you came back home to the golden room, where the sun shines, through night and day, and where tenderness was waiting for you . . . and then you were carried off. . . .
The End.

[4 September, 1901.]
My child thanks you for your tender and beautiful greetings.
Harriet

[About 4 September, 1901.]
Just before your letter came . . . (Think of it! I cannot call you by your first name any longer—that is how far you have strayed from me!)—I went into the bedroom and knelt by your bed, which had already been stripped. I thanked you for all the beautiful and glorious moments you had given me, I begged God that He would protect you and bless you, and I said a prayer for a happy ending to this fairy tale, imploring to be spared from an ugly, bitter ending.

Then came your letter!

I cannot deny that my thoughts, too, had taken the direction that our married life was not necessarily dependent upon living together, keeping house jointly, or even personal contact. You may recall the time I said: "I love you too much."

But how can I be united with your soul when, through you, I must come in close contact with people unknown to me, with strange and unsympathetic souls? I was to be a courtier at your court, as a pastime for you, a subject for conversation in your *pension*. This I cannot be, for I must not be debased!

You speak of my suspicions! I have given voice to no suspicions. I have requested an explanation of certain obscure utterings which have poisoned me, and which were plainly intended as poison, since you could not explain them.

You mentioned, for instance, that I was not a man. What did you mean by that? We did have a child together, didn't we?

You said that you could never again see Rich. B . . . I naturally inquired why, but since you have never given me an answer, I remain in uncertainty of the reason which cannot be a proper one. This should not be called suspiciousness, but your silence can give cause for frightful misunderstandings.

When I had read your letter—I began writing the final lines of *Engelbrekt*. This is my child of sorrow, written with blood and tears . . . It is now finished . . . Think of my sorrow! How glad I would have been to see your eyes glance over these pages . . . You were the first one—it was in Denmark—who saw this drama at its birth, and you read the first act! It is beautiful—it deals with us—with our parting—but grandly and lovely—not a word of hatred, not a smile, no banality . . . Heavy as sorrow, the sorrow of the dead one still living.

But it was too late!

The deranged idea flew through my head to ask you, in the midst of agony, as a consolation, to read it in spite of everything . . . But I can't give my thoughts, my soul away to strangers. . . .

Why should the child bear my name now, after we have parted? My despised, defamed, ridiculed name—which your relatives hesitate to speak and which you refuse to bear?

Lovisa is now packing your belongings, placing them in chests, like corpses—young corpses of memories so young!

This is the bitterest I have ever experienced, for I loved you. . . .

And now remains a hard, heavy task—to bury the memories and to forget you. . . . I labored under the delusion that I would be able to weep out and forget you, but I was mistaken.

My child! It is mine, yet never will be, for when it sees the

light, the mother will be a stranger to me, known by the entire city, but not by me!
The last letter! The last farewell! Forever farewell! How strange!

[*About 4 September.*]
"Forever farewell!" Is it possible? And why? Because I was not kind.
Wasn't I? Did I not suppress my antipathies in order to be pleasing to you? I gave you a grand piano, although I abhor grand pianos; your room was decorated in yellow and green even though I detest these colors; I bought Grieg's music, although he seemed too old fashioned to me; and I asked [you to play] Emil Sjögren in spite of my dislike for him.

I accompanied you to Denmark, the worst land I know; I sat down to table d'hôte, which is a torture; I went in bathing at a sandy beach—something that recurs in my most horrible dreams. I permitted you to hold court at the *pension* and to be attended by cavaliers, whom you yourself spoke of as crude, but I found it impossible to act as cavalier to ladies who had been "engaged" eighteen times. Finally—and there came the break—you tried to force me to admire that ungrateful, faithless disciple [of mine] von Heidenstam. Then I left the room, and for this I may be forgiven. . . .

Was I not kind when I respected the secrets of the yellow room—the part you played in these—when I revered your "secret room," as you called it (and which was not secret), while you at least once a day, with demoniacal pleasure, broke out in admiration and sang the praises of a name that you, as a respectable woman, ought to have avoided mentioning! How could you stoop to such base behavior? It was more cynical than the vulgarity I used and which was not aimed at you, much less at our child—it was merely a supposition that that word might one day be used by mean people about our child!

Why did I not strike back?
Why, because I was kind, because I loved you . . . It was for this reason I kept silent and suffered—for such is love . . . But by so doing, I became used to being reticent and uncom-

municative . . . until, in the end, I felt myself to be false to you. Falseness—that was the result of our married relationship. A volcano of stored-up, suppressed opinions was created, and it had to explode—it did so in Berlin.

I can understand your astonishment after you had lived in self-deceit for four months—self-deceit is the right word!

You were under the impression, namely, that you ruled me because I was silent; you thought that you made an impression on me with your spiteful acts and words, especially when you, during the press week, sat in my sofa and meted out wisdom from the middle of the past century. I accepted this as a trial—Hercules with Omphale—wished to see how long I could tolerate unfriendly rudeness (in elegant form) and you were so attractive to look at when you were malicious—beautiful like a spoiled child which one permits to pull one's hair! I grieved inwardly seeing you and your debasement. . . .

For it was humiliating to see a man who had accomplished what I had in life, being treated irreverently by a girl.

You speak of my delusions! I have never had any others than those you have given me.

Why did you leave? No doubt you were ashamed of some bad act you thought you had sufficient strength of conscience to bear; but on scrutinizing it closer, your robust conscience could not bear up under it!

This is what I believe now. . . .

[*After 4 September, 1901.*]

Beloved,

You say that you would die if you ever came back. This is what you said last spring—and people said: Look, how radiant she is!—I, who saw little Bosse die, divined the resurrection, and—although I suffered—I hoped!

I have seen the Great Woman, my wife, being born in pain, and never have I seen your beauty as I see it now!

You say that you shall become mean and contemptible. No, my dear, your child shall make you good.

Have you not observed that people have grown tired of being wicked, that they long for goodness and beauty! Why do you wish to retrogress—your twenty years into the past?

What is it you wish to go through? On no account is it necessary for you, as mother and as artist, to live through my bachelor life, is it? How shall I otherwise interpret what you say?

Again you say: From now on I shall live only for my child and my art. . . .

Is that feasible? Give your child a home and a father, and give your art a friend, a servant!

Harriet, let me see you once more! I vow not to speak of anything else than our interests in the arts, and to prove to you how glad it will make my heart to see you. I am writing *The Growing Castle*—grand, beautiful, like a dream . . . It is, of course, about you—Agnes—who shall liberate the Prisoner from the castle! . . . What will happen now?

Will you not let me read it into life with you?

How is the little one?—I am going about here like the Sexton on Rån Island, converting ruins into poetry. Yesterday I put the yellow room in order—as it used to look, with the green bed and the blue one underneath the golden circle in the ceiling. And meantime I playfully fancy that the little one is to be born in the green bed, where the violets, embroidered on the nightgown, lie waiting!

When I noticed it, I was gripped by agony, for in that moment I became aware of what I had lost!—Before long I won't be able to indulge in play any more, and then I shall die. . . .

[*7 or 8 September, 1901.*]

My beloved wife,

You see, don't you, that you have returned to my mind . . . and you are here about me, though as a shadow. Some days ago a hope was awakened . . . an angel let me hear a whispered word in my ear—that you merely wished to test me! But by that time the yellow room was broken up—I *had* to save my life by obliterating the memories . . . I then let everything remain—and it is still there—but my blue bed awaits you instead of the green one. . . .

Engelbrekt was requested by the Swedish Theatre, but as I hoped you would come and read it first, I let them wait.

Some one told me that you—as a test—were waiting for me to "beg you" to come back. I answered: I have pleaded in every letter of mine! It could not be expected that I should stand at the telephone; and to risk a visit where I would not be received—*that* I would not dare, for my heart would break!

What, then, are you waiting for? And need you test my love? Need you?

Everything grieves for you: the rooms are weeping—Lovisa hoped to the last—the few who pay me a visit, speak in subdued tones as if in a house of death. Darkness set in when you left. . . .

I can't read any more, can't write; my life is over for me, all interest is gone!

Is it some kind of false pride that fetters you? But you were to take a trip for recreation, weren't you? That is what the physician and we both decided. Let it now come to an end!

Tell me, beloved, that you will return, and I shall put the yellow room in order in the way that you wish—perhaps as it was beforehand . . . And you shall sleep with your little hand in mine and, with new experiences, seek for the best and the most beautiful—avoiding, through small sacrifices, anything that is not harmonious!

You can see, can't you, that I am setting aside my pride; I plead again and again, exposing myself to your humiliating refusals. Won't you greet my little child for me, and won't you write to me what is on your mind now?

Yours

Or may I see you elsewhere? Whatever you wish!

P.S. If you can think of some possibility of conquering your antipathy to me, then let us meet. If you dislike the apartment, then let us meet at the hotel at Saltsjöbaden and remain there a few days!

I shall move and rent out the apartment if its memories are painful to you.

I shall move to Switzerland with you until the child

arrives; and you must take a leave of absence from the theatre!

The child! Yes! Who shall hold your little hand when the child arrives—who shall kiss the fevered brow and suffer with the mother the torment she endures, to alleviate her pains?

September, 1901 [about 8 Sept.].

All is ended: I sense it even as though our child no longer lived. I myself have been near the end—death by my own hand. But I shall make an attempt—to flee! If it is possible to flee from a soul one has been in love with and which is everywhere!

That you cannot care for me is not your fault, my poor friend. The voice that whispered in my ear last Easter Day: "The suffering that is in store for you now will surpass anything you have ever endured!"—that voice was right! But the blame is not yours! It was meant to happen!

Is it advisable that we see each other before I depart?

I would have liked to have thanked you for the greatest joys I have had in many a year, for the mental rejuvenation you brought about, for the longing for beauty that you awakened.

But that I can write—have already written!

If I survive this, well . . . even so it is the end!

Forgive me, then, for enticing you to become my wife; forgive the harsh words—perhaps it was chastisement for your wicked thoughts—I don't know! . . . .

A letter from Harriet Bosse to August Strindberg

[8 September, 1901.]

Dear Gusten,

I was to have written you a long letter, but I have been so very sick, and still am, that I cannot collect my thoughts sufficiently to write a lengthy, explanatory letter until later on.

One thing I can tell you at this time: that I *cannot* return home again—I cannot—I cannot! . . . .
Forgive me, if I hurt you!!!

Harriet

[8 or 9 September, 1901.]

Harriet,
Before I put an end to my torture, in a monastery or otherwise, do write that long letter and give the reason for your being unable to see me again!

With this lone outcry you yourself have again given me poison!

I can forgive all—you know that—but there is one thing I have no right to tolerate!

And there exists only this one reason for our separation!

Free me from the suspicion you have planted in me, and give me back my faith in—the only thing—the last!

You say: "Abandon me!"

This I have no right to do, for I have—as you have—promised before God to be faithful to you in hours of need as in days of happiness.

If you have broken this vow, I am nevertheless still bound by it, for the time being.

I sense that it is the end: I have long felt it! And yet . . . Now I shall die!

[About 10 September, 1901.]

This evening I received a friendly greeting that gives me courage to write this.

On my visit last Sunday I met a complete stranger who made an impression so ghostlike, so irreconcilable and hateful that I fled. Yet I was the bearer of such good news for you—which I shall now communicate to you.

Grandinson had been to see me in the afternoon . . . He inquired why you should not act Emerentia. I told him the reason.

But now *Charles XII* is being advertised for November 30. Will you accept the rôle?—There is still a chance. He further suggested that you make your return in April in *Swanwhite*. Will you act it then?

I also proposed *Simoon*, and the question is still open.

On the other hand, I did not discuss *Mary Stuart*, as I am writing *Queen Kristina* for you—and with an entirely new technique which I especially would have liked to have talked over with you, and to have read it with you.

This is what I had intended to say, but—I became mute—out of grief and fear!

I have painted—I am ashamed to say beautifully—a large canvas representing the Child's First Cradle . . . You see Öresund at sunset with Kullen and Nakkehoved—surrounded by green and flowers, and with a gilt frame. May I present it [to you] for your dressing room?

Forgive me for being unable to live in a room of death with its memories—and for moving into the yellow room. . . .

I wanted to come to grips with memories that were on the verge of doing away with me.

Lovisa, who loves you, says that everything can be put in order in three hours!

[*About 12 September, 1901.*]

To be able to part as friends, there is only one way: to erase and have a clean slate. In other words, to forgive each other, as is the wont between good human beings.

To come with bills and counter bills, as we have been doing, will not do.

I desired to be your friend and was your most faithful one, making it my mission to serve you—but you—you would not permit me!

It is not true that I am selfish! I cannot live without being permitted to give! I have always given—yes, sacrificed!

It is not true that I was left alone because I was a tyrant. I remain alone because I wish to isolate myself from the evil influences of people who are still cast in the mold which I— with so much pain and drudgery—have broken away from.

It is not true that I have a beam in my eye and therefore look at the world with crooked eyes! My eye is a microscopic and magnifying one—that is why I can see farther and more clearly than others. I see that the world is evil, and of this I have had convincing proof recently. But I understand also that we have to put up with it, suffer and endure. For three weeks I have wept . . . from grief over the perishability of all that is beautiful in life . . . To me you were the most beautiful, the loveliest, the purest . . . and then you disappeared.

Today I have wept all day long and felt convinced I would not live until the next spring . . . my heart is affected and my chest is hollow from coughing, especially during the nights.

I have suffered pangs of conscience for refusing to take your little hand when last you offered it to me, and I have reproached myself that I asked you to become my bride. I have grieved over my harsh words, but I had to speak them, as I was in danger of being false to you.

Let me remain your friend! Let me serve you—until the child is born. At that time your feelings will have changed and you can make your choice!

Your position at the theatre is, of course, unpleasant for the moment, and for that I am to blame, having taken you as my wife. Would you prefer to change from *Swanwhite* to *Kristina* for your return to the stage? If so, let me go through this play with you aloud. I am in the midst of the first act, but I wish to have you to dedicate it to. Else it will turn out to be hateful and vile, perhaps ugly! It will be the greatest rôle ever written for a woman. It has an entirely new technique.

Come to see me! We shall discuss nothing but "other things." I am always at home and alone! Should anyone be with me, he will have to leave!
P.S.
  I forgot the last time to give answer to the most alarming reason for your reluctance to start anew.

  You spoke of my imaginings. Beloved, beloved, I have no other imaginings than those you have given me. This you must know!

  And so: if you cannot persuade yourself to return, then

I must go away, far away—for here I shall die out of sorrow and shame. . . .

Thus: everything depends on your one meagre little word: yes or no!

I must go away, for if I remain with my memories, then . . . Yesterday, for the first time, the thought of voluntary exile in death occurred to me, and it grows and is coming to a head!

And then—in a year or two—I shall return home! And then I shall meet a little child's carriage on Strandvägen . . . and if I should ask . . . it is *my* child and it doesn't know me!

But so be it!

My friend!

I cannot be your enemy!

Accept these two remembrances: "The First Cradle" and "The Last Ray of Sun." You may place one of them in a closet and later give it to my child!

I have written to Grandinson and asked that you be given Emerentia as you would help the play by acting that rôle!

The third act of *Kristina* is finished! I shall not change my address before it is completed . . . thus, next week.

After that? . . . Will you read it first? And play in it later?

Your friend
Gusten

20 September, 1901.

A letter from Harriet Bosse to August Strindberg

[*20 September, 1901*]

My dear!

It was so kind of you to remember me with your paintings. I thank you—it gives me much joy to have them!

I awakened last night at exactly two o'clock with the feeling that something was trying to rouse me—and in the light

I saw some roses I had on my bed table bending their heads over me, half dead from tension and tiredness, gazing at me with dry, wide open, weary eyes. . . .

Then I felt my heart beat violently, and an inexplicable anxiety came over me. . . .

I will, of course, be radiantly happy to read *Kristina*. Thank you for entrusting her to me!

Your
Harriet.

21 September, 1901.

My Friend,

Merely to thank you for your letter—to send some roses, which, I am certain, will not gaze at you with dry eyes.

Now I am on the fourth act. Oh, how I miss a table now, at which we could sit and give voice to *Kristina*: especially the end, which is the most important part.

I am having sent to you the manuscript of *Swanwhite*—the original—and ask you to keep it safe in your possession as a remembrance of our so beautifully commenced marriage. You know that the rôle is yours whenever you so desire!

That you are awakened at the stroke of two by palpitation of the heart, and anguish—read *Inferno* and you will understand what it means!

Your Friend
August Strindberg

A letter from Harriet Bosse to August Strindberg

Dear One!

Thank you for the beautiful flowers, which fill the entire room with the most glorious fragrance.

Who do you think can miss more deeply than I our moments at the table, the joy of being with you in your work?

Your Harriet

21 September, 1901.

My dear friend,

In three days or so *Kristina* will be glanced over by your beautiful eyes!

But will you not—in order to be somewhat *au courant*—read something about Kristina before then!

Fryxell is most easily read—almost like a novel—and can be found on Birger Jarlsgatan, where you got *Pickwick,* you remember!

Or something shorter! Odhner?

It has now five complete, well-defined acts. "The greatest and most fundamental female character that has been written!" And five glorious changes of costume, among which Pandora's—out of Walter Crane, you recall—that we planned to use for *Swanwhite.*

I am now collecting the portraits for you! I would like you to look in at the Library and ask to see all the portraits of Kristina.—We shall need only the attractive ones—the pictures from her youth!

The ugly Kristina, Michelson has recently depicted.

What luck for the unfortunate queen that I still possessed the beautiful image of yourself in the portrait I have of you— and [the one] in my heart—now that I have portrayed her! And that you, as an actress, are here with us! (The new century's!)

Have you received *Swanwhite?* We'll let her wait for another year!

Write a few lines now and fortify my interest in the last acts with a friendly word. Let me hear that the little one is alive! (I dreamed last night about a child's severed little foot in the sand!)

Have you received Emerentia?

Are you in good health?—How is *King René's Daughter* doing?—When will *Charles XII* be given now?

                                               Your friend

What a grace from God that I can work! Else—well! Before it was black and dreary—but now . . . even Sorrow itself has become light!

> Two letters from Harriet Bosse to August Strindberg

*Saturday evening [21 September, 1901]
at about ten o'clock.*

Dear One!

On my return home this evening from the theatre (I have been tidying up my dressingroom) I found your kind letter awaiting me.

Your letter made me so eager to learn to know Kristina more intimately that I immediately wanted to borrow the books you recommended, from the lending library. On second thought it occurred to me that all shops were closed at this late hour; but on Monday I hope to be able to quench my thirst for knowledge.

Swanwhite I have not yet received. Possibly people are still in ignorance of my address: whether I am at the Östermalm Pension, at the Möllers', or—with you! . . . .

Our only hope now is *Charles XII*. We are prepared for a mere two, at the most three, performances of *A Desert Tale*. The same goes for *Bianca*.

Palme is surreptitiously practising to look majestic and covers the stage in two enormous strides (the boots!); and the only way to bring a smile of hope to the face of Falck is by mentioning *Charles XII!*

Quite seriously, the interest in your play is so genuine, the anxiousness of the actors to be given even the smallest rôle in it so great that they are all looking forward impatiently to the first rehearsal, the date of which has not yet been fixed. However, it is rumored that the play, in its entirety, will have its première on November 15th. I am still completely without feeling for *King René's Daughter*. Possibly this is because I cannot endure the old-fashioned, stilted language in it. It makes me feel clumsy and unnatural. I am probably being very ungrateful, for everybody says that the rôle is "so sweet."

That dear little child of mine!

It has been so nice, so well-behaved, entirely too well-behaved, that I asked the doctor yesterday what could be the matter.

He smiled at my fears and exclaimed that everything was normal, and that he doubted that a healthier child than mine would ever see the light of day! . . . .

Oh, I am so happy over it! I now believe it will be a boy!

Goodnight, goodnight, my dear, and dream of me and the child!

Harry

Do you really, really long so for me?

This letter was written before I received your latest note. Nevertheless I wish you to read it.

My dear, I shall come whenever you wish me to!

Your
Harriet

Tomorrow forenoon you will see me, if you so wish!

[22 September, 1901.]

I must not be together with you any more for the reason that—should we come together again—you will see it as something unbeautiful. Oh, it is that, of which I am afraid!

And I *cannot* live in an atmosphere of unloveliness or enmity! I simply cannot! Then I would rather tear out my heart with its fresh and comparatively pure memories . . . If I could only know that things would be better on my return! But they will not be!

The next time either one of us expresses a desire, or there is an exchange of opinion between us, the bomb would explode again.

I with my definite ideas and you with yours. Of course, we can give in to each other—to a certain degree.

Only imagine my having to hear again that I drag you down—I who wish for nothing better than to see you at the pinnacle!

I have told you so many times that I am still so far—so far beneath you. Yet I neither can nor will force the normal progression of my nature. This does not mean that I do not understand you; and similarly I expect you to understand me.

And this! There is so infinitely much that is beautiful, in which I still believe, and which I cannot allow to have taken from me. This I have no right to yield in, for that would be an act of ingratitude.

Sometimes an insane desire to break out into laughter—to be happy—to embrace the whole world out of sheer joy—comes over me! This you will scarcely understand. If I should deny myself this feeling, I would wither and die. And hearing me voice such a feeling would only make you unhappy. What, then, is the best way out for us, dear? Dare you take me back after what I have now told you, and—knowing what my view is in this matter—with a promise of understanding, as *I* shall try to understand *you*—then I shall return. O, but, my dear, what a responsibility! The happiness of two beings—all through life! To me this is, indeed, a grave responsibility.

Think on this, my dear, and write me how you feel about it.

I myself think it best that we do not see each other any more! My dear, dear. . . .

Harriet

Sunday

Dearest,

You regret most that you are not *permitted* to sit down together with me. Because of whom are you not permitted? Can you answer me?

You promised not long ago before God to sit at table with me all through life.

And now you are not allowed to!

All these unanswered questions make this fairy tale still more horrible to me!

I shudder now at the thought of the moment when *Kristina* is ready, for then—with nothing to occupy me—I shall break down!

This I shall never be able to survive!

Today a whole month has passed . . . O God, have mercy on me!

22 September, 1901.

P.S. I will not conceal from you that after the impression I received this evening, I felt that my penitence and my sacrificial well-wishes for the child were at an end!

I returned . . . to moderation from asceticism; the suffering for others had served its purpose, and I gave myself absolution!

Tell me! Do you wish to have a farewell celebration! If so, we shall arrange one!

Harriet! Shall we concentrate our efforts on *Kristina* for the spring? You might create it in Germany, in Denmark, in Norway—in Paris (I shall have it translated immediately)!

One word more. To begin with, flee from your *pension;* you will waste away there. Take lodging at the *pension* in Kommendörsgatan, behind Olympia. There is where Schering lived, and it is kept by a German woman.

22 September, 1901.

Harriet,

In heaven's name, let me see you before night falls. I have been so close to death that—it is a miracle that I am alive! O God, God help me!

And *Kristina* nearly went to pieces!

Lovisa is out, I dare not remain! Will you let me see you at the *pension*? I don't suppose you would like to come here! Even if my life were in danger? It is.

Harriet, have pity, I don't want to die!

Your Friend

Be kind and telephone.
56.22.

A letter from Harriet Bosse to August Strindberg

[*23 September, 1901.*]

My dear!

My thoughts go out to you—as ever!

I wish I could wing my way with them into your new abode,

and let you feel all the good I desire for you! That you may find peace and rest from all sad and sick thoughts. . . .

I am sending you greetings from our little child. It has shared my pain this afternoon—as you can well understand.

I went up to Karlavägen this evening to speak with Lovisa—but no one was at home. Closed up, and dark. So dark that I doubt that there ever could be light again.

It is so very strange—all this that is happening.

Goodnight!—I would so like to place my hand on your brow. . . .

The little one sends greetings.

Your own Harriet

Monday evening.
Am reading *Kristina* tonight.

Harriet!

Now I know it! God has given you the power over me—and I submit. But do not misuse this terrible power which is accompanied by responsibility. Use it only for good, and we and our child will benefit from it on this earth. It is true, Harriet, that you literally hold my life in your little hand. If you leave me, I shall die, perhaps by my own hand, or my reason will be destroyed. When I now ask you to come back, you will understand that I am prepared to accept both good and bad from your hand—without complaining. . . .

And what you last told me you had in store for me, I do not believe! For the child, your motherhood, your suffering has—without your realizing it—brought forth a new, a great and glorious woman, of whom I caught a glimpse the last time, and who made me happy!

You once told me about your sister Alma and the change in personality that her motherhood brought about!

This is what is in store for you, too! And the consideration for your child's future shall compel you to hate all evil.

Where is there another married couple with so much in their favor for living life together as we two? Is there any, do you think?

You mentioned last that you looked on your position in my life as a mission! Yes, I believe that! Fulfill then your mission, spur me on and stimulate me to goodness and good deeds and beauty as in the past—and castigate my arrogance with tender cruelty now and then!

I shall kiss your hand, even when it smites, for He who guides your hand is kindly disposed toward me!

Your spirit is with me all hours of the day, and you stand guard over my conscience! Whenever I am tempted to think or write anything unlovely or odious, I see before me your beautiful eyes . . . Then I blush, am ashamed, and correct myself.

I cannot divert myself, and to seek companionship elsewhere would make me feel unfaithful to you—for my soul belongs to you alone. Do not reject my life which I have dedicated to you, for then my death will cast a shadow over your bright path. Forgive me—all, all the wrongs I have done to you!

Sacrifice a little of yourself for me, and I shall sacrifice all for you. I have been unjust to you in the sense that I punished your thoughts when they were not kind!

I had no right to do that. No doubt you have kept innocent little secrets from me! I had no right to delve into them. That is why I was punished by suspicions!

A pleasant, kindhearted person remarked quite rightly: "Perhaps you have asked too many questions!"

I have done that! Forgive me!

And so: What we have now been through, neither you nor I can be blamed for. "It is not the doings of men, but the will of God that has been done."

Therefore, let us cease our accusations and stop seeking the cause!

Come back, my dear! I shall be your servant, I shall obey you—except in what is wrong! I shall serve your child, I shall carry you both in my arms!

And with your presence you shall spare my creative work from hate and unloveliness!

You shall—I am now convinced of this—fulfill your task:

to reconcile me to mankind and woman! Since you have now become woman and mother!
Make the attempt! God will help us!
23 September, 1901.

[*24 September, 1901.*]
Beloved little friend,
Once more I have eluded death! Your kindhearted letter of yesterday, filled with humanity, lay on my bed table and sent forth pious prayers, like incense.

I had made my sacrifice yesterday . . . had left behind the light and cleanliness of Karlavägen . . . stepped into, down into darkness and dust . . . but God was with me. There was a piano school on the premises, they were practising on brass instruments, people were beating rugs . . . but I felt no annoyance for I was prepared for the worst—I had given, given all that I possessed! And peace came to me! I had a calm night!

But then I awakened in the morning: And then I felt the whole weight of the humiliation . . . and can you imagine, I had the impression I was at the *hôtel garni* where Jörgensen's Eva stopped [once]—you recall the sofa with the four loose legs! The closet smelled of carbolic acid—as if someone had committed suicide there—other people's belongings were mixed with mine—the wash basin, in which I dipped my face, was filthy. . . .

So I fled here! Here I shall die—in light, in cleanliness—be able to see the woods, the sea, and the sky—and, in company with your bright little tender spirit which still hovers about—enjoy your companionship to the end. Thus: The apartment is still here, and I shall watch over it!

Come and sit here by our clean dining-room table and speak about *Kristina!*

I had a frightening feeling this morning that you disliked the play—that I had overestimated it . . . and that you were angry with me!

Then the Eumenides took hold of me again, and I wanted to die!

And then I fled here! Here is light, cleanliness, a friendly atmosphere!

Your
Gusten

Bring [your copy of] *Kristina*, please, and I shall promptly purge it of slag.

26 September, 1901.

Harriet,

Yesterday I had a definite feeling that you had happened into a blind alley—in other words, very much as I had. To go forward is impossible, to retrogress is undesirable—thus the only way out is to climb over the wall!

And so: Come along with me to Switzerland—tomorrow! Ask for a leave of absence!

I shall have the rôles in *Swanwhite*, *Kristina* and *Simoon* written out! You can be studying these with the expectation that they will be produced next spring! At any rate one of them! For the rest, you can do some sculpturing, read some novels, help me to give voice to my dramas!

The apartment we will keep until January 1. If you then still find it odious, we will dispose of it! And if you should feel—after the child has been born—that you can resume your marital life with me, then I shall furnish an apartment . . . shall let Axel furnish it while we are away.

And then we could take possession of it in May—with our child! By that time you and I will be new human beings! Are you willing?—

asks
Your faithful friend
Gusten

26 September, 1901.

P.S. Personne was given *Kristina* at nine o'clock this morning.

[*About 2 October, 1901.*]

Beloved!

Is it the end of this beautiful dream that is approaching? Can there be an end to it—and why should there be? I am with you with my soul day and night, there are no distances between us. Life has no interest except through you, and if the dark shadow of the feeling of my loss did not appear, the memory of you would make up for it!

You were to me not a human being but an apparition . . . Your bright, tender little spirit spread light in the darkness; and as I now gaze at the portrait of Puck framed by magic flowers, I see a good-natured child hankering to play troll and to be wicked, but failing in this pastime.

When I regarded your regal beauty—at the seashore—I trembled at the thought of my boldness, my presumption, to have dared to covet you, and I felt a fear that the world—the whole world—envied me! It was too much for me . . . I was shamed—and I was frightened!

How miraculous, Harriet, that after I had wept clean *my* soul for forty days, Swanwhite returned to me again! And thus she came to you, too—and now your and my Swanwhite shall be wedded in the purity of your love!

"God has kissed together our hearts," you said! Then why should he separate us?

Is it the little one* who strives to bring up its parents to be worthy parents . . . to a generation of the new century, to the coming mankind?

Or was it I who destroyed my happiness when I awakened you, little sleepwalker? The self-accusations—oh!

What will happen now?

3 October, 1901.

My beloved little wife,

After our conversation this evening I felt convinced not only that you cannot return to the apartment—since you prefer four hours in the street—but that you and I can live life—in gypsy tradition, however. I was the first to hate "the apartment"—I, the son of the hut and the hovel—the son of the servant girl—of Hagar—of the desert! . . . .

Accompany me on the pilgrimage into the desert, beloved! You were my child, my daughter—now, mother! Now I am

* Their as yet unborn child.

your child! As you so beautifully said: "You, Gusten, lie under my heart!"—And it was my *Inferno* dream to fall asleep on the breast of a woman!

But when you this evening mentioned that the little one had my eyes—as it was sleeping in your arms . . . as you once slept in mine . . . then all became different! The past erased!

Let me arrange (I wrote to Personne this evening) for you to play Iolantha as your farewell performance before your departure!

Or—free yourself from the Royal Theatre and make your re-entrance as Kristina with Ranft in April? Or—whatever you desire!

Would you like to go to Paris—with me? You may live in a *pension* if you would like that!

You may keep house, with Lovisa, in Paris, if that is what you prefer!

You could have a suite of rooms in a hotel. Whatever you desire! Give all this a thought—all except the apartment! That goes!

And leave your return to the stage in my hands! The autumn and winter in Paris, learning French—the only language worth being learned by us!

Let me be such as I am until our child has arrived! Then—will be the time for you to make your decision for the future.

              Your Gusten

Beloved Wife,

Forgive me for leaving you in that manner—but I simply lost my head! Forgive me!

Last night I slept in the blue bed—and fumbled for your little hand in the darkness!

Today the sun is shining and the apartment wears a smile! Come at noon and read again *The Man in the Corridor*—which will then be finished!

My thanks for yesterday! I asked too much!

                Your
                Gusten

5 October, 1901.

[On October 6 that year (1901) Harriet Bosse returned to her and Strindberg's home on Karlavägen in Stockholm. There she and Strindberg waited for the birth of their child. Harriet Bosse describes Strindberg's touching attentions to her during this period and the interest he took in her career, his plans for her in the future and his efforts to teach her foreign languages and to encourage her in her musical studies.]

With never waning patience he kept after me in my study of languages. He wanted to see me act not only on the Swedish stage, but abroad as well. His idea was that I perfect myself first in German in order to be able to appear on the stage in German-speaking countries. However, I was happy at the Royal Theatre. The rôles allotted to me were to my liking, and I had no reason whatever to complain. Besides, I was no doubt somewhat lazy, and to act in a foreign language seemed to me to be an insurmountable obstacle.

While waiting for my little Anne-Marie to come into the world, Strindberg was constantly considerate and thoughtful of me. Once in a while he could not refrain from touching upon the delicate question of women's rights. The hairs on his upper lip would bristle, I would burst into tears—and then he would go over to a wash basin in his room and wash his hands hastily, nervously, again and again, as was his habit when he was agitated over something. And then the storm was over. . . .

A touching characteristic of his, which I especially recollect from this time, when waiting for Anne-Marie to come, was this: I could not bear the odor of cigarette smoke; and as Strindberg smoked a good deal, I suffered greatly as a consequence. He noticed this, and gave up smoking for several weeks, until I was able to tolerate it again. He had a little cabinet in the foyer, and in this he locked all his smoking articles. He called it his "poison cabinet"!

Strindberg liked to hear me play. He showed a preference

for Grieg's sonata in C minor and Beethoven's sonatas, Schumann, Schubert and Peterson-Berger. He himself played the piano rather well. I could occasionally hear him carefully feeling his way through, among other compositions, Gounod's *Romeo and Juliet* and *Faust* and a few of the less difficult passages from some sonata by Beethoven, his favorite composer.

Little Anne-Marie was born in the spring of 1902, on the very Day of the Annunciation. This brings to mind an episode that occurred on that eventful day. One of my sisters, who was staying with me, had read that Strindberg had declared in his writings that childbirth was nothing but pleasure for women. When my pains were at their worst, she opened the doors to the rest of the apartment, in which Strindberg was walking nervously to and fro. No sooner had my sister opened the door leading to my room than Strindberg shut it. This maneuver went on for quite some time; and no matter how much I suffered, I could not help but smile through my tears.

As he had previously promised in 1901, so again he promised that we would spend the approaching summer in the country. We discussed from time to time where we might find a suitable place to live. Our opinions differed, and I was afraid that—when the time came and a decision had been made—Strindberg would, after all, not leave Stockholm. Having always loved nature, I longed to break away from the city and the confinement of the somber apartment on Karlavägen.

If at one time or another I complained to him about my loneliness, he would remark: "How can you talk about being lonely? When you appear on the stage, you are among comrades, aren't you? And, besides, you have the whole audience with you, haven't you?" As time passed, and we were still rooted in Stockholm, I determined to take my little daughter with me and go to Rävsnäs, a domain of the Crown, in Lake Mälar, where I had spent a year as a child.

The following letter was placed in my room, while I was out. Anne-Marie and I were to leave for the country the next day. Judging by this letter, it seems as if Strindberg had desired to come with us to Rävsnäs. I had pleaded with him time and time again to join us; but he had always refused. Therefore I took it for granted that he preferred to remain in Stockholm.

[*July, 1902.*]

Faced with the inevitable, I am struck dumb and petrified . . . I no longer believe it possible to dissuade you from leaving; you will most likely persist in your decision—and whether this is a passing test or a judgment on me, I cannot know. But I feel as though I will not be able to survive it. While I have suffered all the tortures of our separation for the past three months, the worst pain is yet to come. . . .

The child kept me alive and bound me to you. . . .

What our disagreements were about, I cannot remember . . . Therefore they must have been mere bagatelles; perhaps an exaggerated solicitude for the little one and a pardonable anxiety.

That you regretted the loss of your girlhood I could understand. But I had hoped that the child would bring back your youth to you—as it did to me . . . But no!

At this moment I have nothing to reproach you with. Married life brings with it a certain constraint. Just as you no doubt have at times longed to be free from such restraint, so have I—and I have hoped that I again might hold the lone center of interest in my circle. But I soon realized that this was merely a fanciful dream. My friends have become indifferent strangers to me through your presence in my life. And I can feel that complete isolation is on the way—awesome, dismal and solemn. . . .

Last evening I had intended to ask you—frankly, straightforwardly: "Why may I not come with you to Rävsnäs? Why do you wish to send me off to Sandhamn to parade my grief before strangers?"—But the words froze on my lips.

What will happen now, I do not know. I assume I shall remain in the only hiding place I have, my dream castle. No matter what may happen, I shall not touch the furnishings. Whatever you may wish to have, remains at your disposal.

When I ran unto the howling northwind today, this thought occurred to me momentarily: "Is it possible that this fate can escape me—that the inevitable is not inevitable?"

When you one morning some time ago pleaded with me from the depth of your soul: "Help me!" I interpreted it in this manner: "Help me to flee from this home—to flee to freedom!" As this most easily could be accomplished through my departure—which would mean my ruin—I thought you wished me to leave. But that you should ask me to extirpate myself—that I found hard to accept; and I replied harshly. Since then I have had doubts as to whether you really meant to be so cruel to me. And I have come to feel—perhaps because of my distress and agony—that I would like to interpret your cry for help in this way: "Ask me to forgive you—and I shall forgive! I desire to remain with you, but I cannot until you have helped me!" However, I was probably mistaken . . . Yet if that is what you meant, I say: "Forgive me for misjudging you!"

My feelings for you and our little one are entirely unchanged, even though the horror of our separation paralysed me . . . Can you imagine the torture in store for me—the torture that began already before our child arrived—when you first intimated that you were leaving. In the beginning I intended not to let myself be too deeply attached to the child, in order to suffer less afterward . . . but the little dear one was irresistible.

And now I am alone!

Alone! For you were my oracle! Through your eyes *only* I saw the world—only through you did I keep in touch with the earth. Do you realize that I now may disintegrate in my loneliness: "I obeyed you and things went well for me . . ." You were given the power over me by Providence—but only the power for good! When I felt that you were about to misuse your power, I had to disobey you! That is why I find it difficult to reproach myself for making resistance. I had to hold my head above water—I had to keep myself from going down . . . and for this you will one day be grateful to me! For if I had not, I would have pulled you down with me . . . And that I could never do!

Is your mission in my life now at an end? Is it possible that there can really be an end to all that which we thought had no beginning?

Is Chrysaëtos dead? And are not our souls immortal—no matter what?

[Letter to Rävsnäs:]

4 *July*, 1902.

My beloved wife,

At first it was quiet, of course, as after an earthquake accompanied by a thunder clap . . . but then it grew to be a little too quiet, and I missed your restless little spirit's pit-a-pat on the floor, I missed seeing the open doors, and—perhaps most of all—I missed the little outcries from the nursery.

But when I think of how hopelessly frightful the feeling of loss would have been if we had parted as enemies yesterday, then I am happy; and the peacefulness has the refreshing effect of a rest.

I had contemplated looking for new faces, but I am afraid of obliterating the vision of you, and to fall back again into prehistoric times on Banérgatan. It would reveal a lack of faith in you—even though I know that you are surrounding yourself with your own circle, all strangers to me, where you are now. And in my aloneness I have you with me; but with others around you, you disappear from view, and the contact ceases.

What was our disagreement about? Yes—about keeping our own individuality when we were in danger of melting into one. You held the advantage because you had friends . . . I was completely alone, captured by you and the little child. It made me feel horror-stricken at times, having surrendered myself so unconditionally to you. I wanted to flee, but I could not. All this is quite natural, as natural as that love has a seeding and a blossoming time. One yearns for the seed, but feels the loss of the flower when the seed has come. C'est la vie—qu'est-ce-que vous voulez?

Therefore: If you can find a place for me (and Bertha), just say the word! To continue a useless struggle against the laws of life is folly! The practical thing would be to rent an apartment now, with six rooms, and to give up the months that remain here, moving into a new domicile, where you can have your own room. . . .

. . . . And from then on let us cease philosophizing over our relationship; let us merely occupy ourselves with our work and devote the rest of our efforts and solicitude to our little one.

Give a kiss to my daughter now! Rest your tired nerves! And let us continue our pilgrimage!

These are my feelings now. . . .

Your little husband
Gusten

P.S. The money from Norway is here. Do you want it?

The following letter, sent to Rävsnäs and postmarked 5 July, was accompanied by the manuscript of *The Hollander*:

[5 July, 1902.]

Read the accompanying and you will see what feelings you inspired in me when last I saw you. This was written the day after you left.

And the next day I sent you my friendly letter, in return for which I received your unreasonable one.

[Another letter to Rävsnäs]

12 July, 1902.

Dear Wife,

Welcome, then! But tell me definitely when, and do not change your mind—for the previous time I had made such handsome preparations for your arrival—and then you did not come . . . The green room has been redecorated and made still more beautiful. It is now friendlier than ever. Let me know whether you are coming at noon or in the evening, so that I can receive you worthily—with a sumptuous repast, which you perhaps will need . . . And I must have flowers for you, too!

There is much news that I have to tell you, little items as well as more important matters, both about people and things. *Swanwhite* is to be given at the Lessing Theatre this fall! (Would you like to act the title rôle?)

Yesterday I saw on the street car a little white-clad baby whose head was swathed in bandages. It made me feel so sad; and I thought of our own little one. . . .

Your friend
Gusten

During my stay at Rävsnäs, Strindberg sent, besides *The Hollander*, several other poetic works in manuscript form. Among them were *The Poet's Reward* and *Chrysaëtos*. After a visit of mine in our home in Stockholm, he wrote:

20 July, 1902.

Beloved,

Yesterday was a wonderful day but too short. Today I have heard in my ear so many things I had wished to say but did not find the time to say. . . .

The sorrow of losing you was succeeded by a dull stillness. I felt that we ought to remain away from each other a little longer . . . but I feel strongly that our bond cannot be broken. That I have not grieved to death over our little one, I consider a grace. . . .

Rävsnäs, I fear, I shall never see . . . It is yours, and you must keep it for yourself. It is a setting created for you! But you, who like to travel, must come in to me again—but the next time for a longer visit!

Do you remember the Italian villa of stone out in Djurgården, on the right side of the road, where the dilapidated old Burmeister houses are situated . . . and which I have shown you so many times? It is called the Weylandt Villa . . . I am thinking of taking a lease on it. It would be ideal: perfect southern exposure, and a view of the sea . . . And plenty of room—we won't crowd each other!

What a wonderful day, yesterday! How fortunate for *The Hollander!*

Your
Gusten

I feel certain Strindberg was heartsick for me and our little Anne-Marie. Alone in the city, his solitude lay heavily on him, and he yearned to be with us in the skerries. However, this never came about. The rift had already set in. I felt myself caught and caged; he considered it entirely natural that I should remain in my home. This might very well be only right, but as an artist I felt it to be part of my profession to move about and to see new faces. We both had strongly individual characters, and—young though I was—I had, unfortunately, views and ideas of my own. This did not help matters. Today*—after having passed through much in life— I can see how unreasonable and foolish I was, not to settle down in peace with this man, who asked for nothing better than to be given the opportunity to care for me. Unquestionably it was occasionally somewhat of a hardship to accommodate myself to his changing whims and moods, and to accept his views of life. But if I had erased my own personality and tried to adapt myself to his demands, this might have been possible. Yet, even so, it would be questionable whether things might have been better that way . . . I have a feeling that Strindberg revelled in meeting with opposition. One moment his wife had to be an angel, the next the very opposite. He was as changeable as a chameleon.

Strindberg was kind and warmhearted. He was never ill-natured and fierce as he sometimes depicts himself in his

---

* Harriet Bosse's commentaries were written for the first volume of letters published in 1932.

writings. Only when he took pen in hand did a demon take possession of him . . . and it was this demon that helped to release his genius. Strindberg has both said and written that I probably was the one who best understood him. Whether I did or not, I do not know; nor do I know whether anyone could ever have understood him. I think that he in his youth stretched out his arms toward all the fair and beautiful things that life holds in promise for the young. Later, having discovered that things did not go according to his expectations, and that all the beautiful promises held out to him, had failed of fulfillment, he imagined that he alone had been cheated. It was for this reason he raged in righteous indignation and fury against the world's deceit and its betrayal of him.

His personal feeling of resignation was merely momentary. He lacked the balance for it. He would suddenly fly into yet another rage. To his very last breath he fought against his own Karma.

What probably contributed most to keep us apart was the great difference in our ages. Strindberg, on one hand, had already lived his life and had completed a considerable part of his purpose and aims, while I had scarcely begun my life. The many burning questions—which I was eager to air and discuss—he sidestepped; or he would reject them as something he had already examined and proved wanting, through personal experience.

Much has been said about Strindberg's ingratitude to his friends. I cannot express myself with any intimate knowledge on this subject, since so few of his friends were frequent guests in our home during this period. However, I can recall one time, when he had persuaded himself to attend a dinner party, given for us both, at the home of an acquaintance of his, incidentally not a friend.

The entire gathering was in excellent humor, Strindberg not least. In other words, a most agreeable company; and Strindberg seemed very contented with the evening on our return home. Imagine my astonishment when I, several years later, read in a book of his then just published (*Black Banners, 1907*) with what infernal spite this dinner party had been arranged: Everyone present was a malicious person and the party a complete failure! I presume he wrote this in his loneliness, changing the mood of that evening to suit his own feelings at the time.

It goes without saying that I often suffered from his suspiciousness. It was foolish of me, of course, to take it so to heart. I should have realized that he himself suffered still more deeply.

Once he hurt my feelings unforgivably. I had just given birth to my little daughter. After having gone about in my deformed condition for months, I rejoiced in returning to slender proportions and to be able to wear attractive clothing again. My dressmaker had made me a white cloak, in which I thought I looked very well. I went into my husband's room to show myself to him. His brow wrinkled ominously, and he asked me if I had bought it "to walk the streets in." To weep for words like that may seem childish—but I cried copiously.

I recall to mind an incident that happened to Ellen Key. She arrived one day while we were at table. Strindberg was holding little Anne-Marie in his lap. Ellen Key was announced. Strindberg rose, and—with the words: "I shall receive her"— he handed Anne-Marie to me. From the foyer I heard a few short but strong words—and then he came dashing in furiously, exclaiming: "I threw her out!" Horrorstricken I asked him what had happened. He told me that she had come to ask whether I would like to participate in the program being arranged in honor of Björnstjerne Björnson's seventieth birthday. Strindberg did not wish me to appear—he was afraid of losing me!

The following day I naturally walked over to see Ellen Key and to apologize for the strange reception she had received from Strindberg. This I did not dare tell him, of course. When I had rung the bell I could hear Ellen Key unhook the safety chain. I was forced to smile. Exactly as in our apartment. Ellen Key was understanding and realized what had happened. She spoke of him not only with admiration but with friendliness. And she invited me to have a glass of Italian wine and some ginger cakes.

Strindberg was extremely good to the poor. Never did I see a needy person leave our home without being helped. One morning, returning from his usual early walk to Djurgården, he told me he had encountered an old woman sitting by the road, stretching out her hand to passers-by, begging for a coin. It was a cold morning and the old woman was freezing. She had asked Strindberg if he could give her a blanket; and so I had to go out and buy one for her. The next day he took it with him and gave it to the woman.

The daily morning walks between seven and nine were practically the only outdoor exercise that Strindberg took. He would rise at half past six, brew his own coffee on a Russian coffee urn, and then set off promptly on the road toward Djurgården. It was during these walks he planned and sketched his work for the day. He could take these walks in peace and quiet, as Djurgården was almost entirely asleep at this hour of the day. The few persons he met did not disturb him; they were mostly retired army and naval officers or government officials, for whom life and work were nearly at an end, whiling away the hours until the time came to leave this earth.

On these morning walks he would sometimes get a glimpse of a headline in a newspaper in some window. If this related to some dramatic event or occurence, it might be made to serve as a basis for some incident in one of his works. Strindberg otherwise was not an avid reader of newspapers. In discussing a criticism of one of his premières, he once remarked: "If I had had tremendous praise in eleven newspapers in Berlin, and the twelfth critic did not like the play, you may be certain that the newspapers in Stockholm would quote the twelfth critic." He had a dislike for humorous magazines. "If you enjoy and laugh over a caricature of someone, you may be certain that when you turn the page, you will see one of yourself even more ridiculous and malicious," he would say.

On arriving home from his walk, he would immediately seat himself at his writing table, charged with intensity and ready to work. From then on he would write furiously, feverishly, smoking his Finnish cigarettes. Generally he would have the outline and the dialogue clear in his mind before he commenced to write; this accounts for the very few changes in his manuscripts. While he was at work, no one was permitted to disturb him—i.e., no one but myself. At noon he took a brief pause, after which he set to work again. The afternoons he would spend reading, preparing for the next day's task. He never wrote in the afternoon.* When evening came, he would walk back and forth in the apartment, although mostly round the dining-room table, and up and down in that room. In order to walk softly and with ease, he would wear white rubber-soled shoes indoors.

This pacing about in our apartment often comes to my mind, when I think of Strindberg. He moved with youthful buoyancy as he went from one room to another with Anne-Marie on his shoulder, her little head bouncing hither and thither. Now and then he would come to a halt and take a sip from his whisky and soda glass on the buffet. In parentheses I might say that Strindberg was exceedingly moderate in his drinking of strong liquor.

Strindberg was no gourmet. He preferred simple, well prepared everyday fare. But he disliked seeing people eat. He thought it an ugly sight. He liked to see me surrounded by fruits, flowers and wine. But when the need for other food

---

* Strindberg's habit at this particular period of his life.

occasionally had to be satisfied, it almost seemed as if he apologized for being obliged to eat.

The so-called Beethoven evenings in our home are other memories. That was when the "Beethoven cronies" gathered. During my time the circle consisted of, besides Strindberg, the painters Richard Bergh and Karl Nordström, professor Carlheim-Gyllensköld and my husband's brother Axel, who provided the music. I generally sat crouched in a chair in a corner of the room, where I could watch the "old men" undisturbed. What devotion—and what quiet! And Strindberg—the giant of the assembly—seemed to grow in stature while the music was being played. He assumed to me even more the appearance of a giant: I could see how the music lifted him into other realms, how he revelled in it and was inspired by it. When the musicale was over, a light supper was served. The spirit of these gatherings was always most pleasant; and Strindberg himself exuded charm and friendliness.

Perhaps the following little episode can best illustrate how boyishly exuberant Strindberg could be. He had the sudden notion one evening to serenade Mathilda Jungstedt, the famous opera singer, who lived next door. He was about to go down in the street with his guitar and move into position beneath her window, then to sing the only number he knew, "Jönköping Match Company—patented paraffin safety matches," a popular tune of that day. When I begged and pleaded with him to forgo the serenade, or at least not to bring along his guitar, he took it into his head to accompany his ditty by drumming on an over-size match box—a whim that to me was even more distasteful. People would have thought him demented . . . The serenade did not take place!

Some Strindberg authorities, and as well a great many of the public, hold the opinion that Strindberg was mentally unbalanced. This depends upon what is meant by mental illness. If a person during life's trials should become highly sensitive, shy and suspicious, this need not come under the heading of what is commonly called mental illness.

Such moods frequently took hold of Strindberg. Because his nature was so infinitely complex and subtle, he more easily fell pray to emotions and impressions. The honest compulsion that drove him to turn himself inside out brought upon him the accusation that he was not in his right mind. Others would perhaps conceal their peculiarities deep in their heart—but Strindberg bared his to the world. I have never seen any indication of mental illness in Strindberg; but I was conscious of his individual eccentricities.

During the early days of our marriage I was quite often troubled by the changeability of his moods. Yet I feel certain that Strindberg himself suffered most from his own nature.

Strindberg was far from a woman hater. He adored women. But he felt woman's place was in the home. As soon as she encroached on the domain of the male, she toppled from her pedestal....

Strindberg had such fear of a woman's power over him that he would refuse to see a lady caller, if he knew she was beautiful. I recall one time when Marika Stiernstedt was coming to visit him—the visit, somehow, did not take place! He was afraid she was too beautiful! Nor did he dare face Olga Raphael (Mrs. Linden) who at that time was quite young. She also was too dangerously beautiful! I believe that Strindberg was afraid he might be unfaithful to me, even in thought; and in order not to risk that, he chose to shield himself against any possible temptation.

Did Strindberg have a sense of humor? No—not in the usual sense. His satire was brilliant, but he scarcely enjoyed what is commonly called an amusing story.

I have elsewhere commented on Strindberg's firm belief that he had made gold. He took a much greater pride in his scientific discoveries than he did in being a great author. On the inside of the door of a cabinet in his study he had tacked a page of *Le Figaro,* on which his alchemy experiments were seriously described in a two-column article. He showed it with pride and declared that he was a greater scientist than author.

While we were married, Strindberg did not attend any plays, with two exceptions. We sat hidden in a loge at the Swedish Theatre, witnessing *Old Heidelberg,* with Anders de Wahl and Astri Torsell in the two leading rôles. Strindberg was so moved that he wept. The second play we saw was at the Östermalm Theatre: Strindberg's own *Lucky Per's Journey,* in which his daughter Greta acted Lisa's rôle. Strindberg beamed with pride, both at his daughter's acting and at his play. We took Anne-Marie with us to the theatre. She was only three years old then.

Whenever I was acting in a play for the first time, or when Strindberg himself had a première, he would be pacing nervously back and forth in the apartment. He generally asked to be informed of the outcome, act by act. After I made my first appearance as Juliet in Shakespeare's *Romeo and Juliet,* Tor Hedberg—whom he valued highly as a critic—had made some rather uncomplimentary remarks about my performance. A few days later, however, Hedberg came to see me a second time; and then he wrote a quite beautiful and encouraging review. Beaming, Strindberg brought the newspaper with the criticism to me in my room in the morning. He appreciated that Hedberg had shown so much interest in me that he had troubled to see the performance a second time.

Strindberg showed unfailing interest in my work. He consoled me when the critics disapproved of me, his eyes gleamed like sunlight whenever I was successful. Unquestionably he over-estimated my artistic ability; yet I can truthfully say that his admiration never caused me to have an exaggerated opinion of myself. It merely spurred me on and encouraged me to become what he already thought me to be

An injury to my sense of justice has always offended me more than anything else. When Strindberg violently attacked women's rights or tried to assail what to me seemed just and logical, I protested strenuously. I realized that these wearing dissensions could not continue forever. In order to be able to attend to my duties at the theatre, I would have to live alone. Nevertheless we agreed—after my return from Rävsnäs and Äpplar Island in the summer of 1902—to try to live together still another year. The prospects then seemed somewhat brighter. I had a busy season at the theatre. One important rôle after another took up my time, and I had literally none to spare for pondering my misfortune.

In the spring of 1903 Anne-Marie and I, together with a sister of mine, went out to Blid Island to spend the summer there. As usual, Strindberg remained in Stockholm. But, strangely enough, this summer he came out to visit us at the island. He wished to see whether he would like it there well enough to prolong his stay.

We welcomed him at the pier—my sister, her son (then twelve years old), and myself with Anne-Marie in my arms. Then the little caravan trudged to the modest cottage. Unfortunately we lived rather close upon each other; but there was a still unfinished room in the attic—and this Strindberg decided to use as his study. He had brought with him some Oriental hangings, and these he hung on the walls. It was a habit of his always to have a touch of color to look at while working. However, he could not have felt completely at home on Blid Island, for his stay was a brief one; and he returned to Stockholm.

In the fall of 1903 I moved into a furnished apartment with my little daughter. But Strindberg and I still kept in contact with each other. He frequently came to see us; and habitually Anne-Marie and I would dine with him on Sundays. In this manner the daily dissensions and difficulties were avoided; we met in holiday mood and in a spirit of joy. Occasionally Strindberg felt his loneliness bitterly. When this feeling overcame him, I would receive such letters as the following one:

[25 August, 1903.]
How I have it? Imagine yourself being torn away from your child—and then think!

Imagine my restlessness the nights you are at the theatre and our little one is abandoned to some stranger who has not the slightest interest in children and looks simply to her own convenience. And think—if the child, which by now has forgotten me, should again become acquainted with me . . . and then be torn away once more—and feel the loss of me . . . Do you know what it means to feel the loss of some one and mourn that loss? If you do, you can imagine the anguish she would feel in her little heart!

What do you want of me? You are now free and can enjoy the peace and happiness you did not have at my side. Haven't you realized that I was the cause of your unhappiness?

Catch hold of your happiness, the joy that I denied you—but let me keep my sorrow pure. Follow your fate, which you believe you can govern; but do not touch mine, which is ruled by another power—The One you do not know!

The situation of living apart could not continue indefinitely. We would either have to live together again, or be divorced. We decided to seek a divorce. These continual marital disagreements and dissensions, together with the great strain of my work at the theatre, caused me to have a nervous breakdown. I was compelled to interrupt my acting in *A Venetian Comedy*, which was being played to packed houses in the spring of 1904, and had to move to Saltsjöbaden to seek to recover my health at the seashore. There I was confined to bed for three weeks. All my illusions were shattered. . . .

My sincere desire to bring happiness to Strindberg—to reconcile him to mankind and woman—had failed dismally. I was so deeply fond of him that I found it hard to go through with the operation—the divorce. But it had to be done for the sake of us both, in order to give us peace. However, no actual steps were taken immediately. I longed to get away from Stockholm, for my thoughts kept spinning round and round . . . and I determined to go to Paris for a few weeks. I was broken down mentally and physically.

Among the following letters, the first one was sent to Saltsjöbaden, the second one to my address in Stockholm. Several of the letters were placed by Strindberg in my mail box and are not dated.

Harriet,
    Should you ask me why I did not wish you a [happy] New Year, my answer will be: I did so in my heart the entire New Year's Day.
    Should you further ask why I did not come to you, I must answer: I do not know!
    I do not know why I flee from your home when I visit you; I don't know why I feel animosity when you show friendliness in a particular way.
    You betrayed me once to my enemies. You bore my head on a platter, and my heart in a bowl to these gentlemen of the world, and therefore things can never [again] be as they were! To be friendly with one's enemy? How could one?
    Do not touch my fate with wanton hands! How often didn't I warn you? But you—in your arrogance—had to do it—like the rest!
    I wept for forty days over your betrayal, when you, in front of all the world, mocked him whose only desire was to elevate you. Your determination is to go downward, while I strive toward the heights! You cannot follow me, and I will not follow you! That is undoubtedly the secret!
                      My name
(that was given me by mother and father, and which you could never pronounce.)
1 January, 1904.

[10 *April*, 1904.]
My friend,
So you think that a mere lawyer can accomplish what we ourselves have tried to do but failed in. Or, if you feel the bond is so hard to tolerate, then let it be severed . . . although I can't help feeling that you have used your freedom without regard for it. The marriage vow failed to bind us together; and now you think that a divorce will keep us apart . . . Well, so be it! I—who have felt myself bound by my vow—might gain by it. I shall then feel free to surround myself with whomsoever I wish—to furnish my home as I see fit—to keep any servant I like—to think and act as I please, without fear of criticism from anyone. It will mean that I shall regain my personal independence. And my honor, too, which you now hold in your hand—for if you behave badly, then I shall suffer the dishonor of it. Everything you say about me is accepted as the truth itself—even if it should not be true. That is why you could murder me with a word—if I had not placed my fate in God's hand. I was on the verge of answering you once, when you misused the power, Providence had given you over me, with the words that Christ spoke to Pilate: "Thou could'st have no power at all against me, except it were given thee from above."
You had been given the power over me, but you misused it. You thought it your own power—and that is why it was taken from you. . . .
As to our last disagreement, your suspicions poisoned me to such a degree that I became suspicious myself; and—in looking back on the past—lo, it was filled with deceit, and my emotional life was entirely adulterated. I believe you are now suffering from remorse. This has been my Way of the Cross. All that I experienced with you has now crumbled and turned to ashes. . . .
You will understand how I long for freedom, for honor regained, and restitution. . . .
Very well, so be it!

27 May, 1904

Beloved,

Does one not act rightly by following one's innermost feelings, especially when they bid you act with justice?

Is not this a strong enough sign of our attraction for each other, despite our differences?

And is not our little child entitled to some consideration from us?

You have qualms about taking the trip abroad. Indeed, you should, for you will realize how much our child will miss you. You may even have your journey interrupted and be forced to spend the summer in a hospital in a strange country, far away from us. I can't help feeling that this might happen.

You ask me for advice! Here is some! I will present to you my beautiful Isola Bella at Furusund. Take along a cook and Sigrid. I shall remain in the city with my servant; and will come out and stay with you as long as you wish, or as long as we can endure each other.

We can do this, if we avoid the dangers; and we know what they are. Just as you must have your acting career to yourself, so I must have my writing to myself. Nothing in common but our home, our child and our friends. If each one of us has separate friends and acquaintances, we draw away from each other and become faithless.

Alf and Inez, whom I otherwise am fond of, have a disturbing influence on our life. Let them visit you, when I am in the city.

But we must live as married people, for I am in love with you, body and soul; and I know that we understand each other, even though it took time—as I told you the first night we were together.

And we have to risk having a child, but this time we must try to have a son, so that you won't be disappointed afterward. I now believe that we, after our long abstinence, will have one. And I believe that—as I also long for the beauty you seek—you shall find what you have been in search of for so long.

Let us tempt fortune once again!

What will the world and the lawyer say? They will rejoice in their hearts.

For humanity weeps when it sees the end of a love—even though humanity has no love for those who suffer. . . .

Undated [1904].

I am speechless! I just cannot write business letters to one whom I have worshiped. To worship idols is forbidden, but I have done it—and therefore I am being punished.

If I could speak with you, I could explain my letter and make it clear to you that it is not my opinion, but gossip—brought about by your thoughtless behavior.

A week ago you came with light and peace—and now? . . .

I hear that our little child is ill. And you keep her from me when she needs me!

Do not wrong her, who is innocent—for she, too, has someone watching over her. . . .

Our home is entirely at your disposal. After you moved out, I no longer care to see it. It no longer holds any attraction for me!

Come and let us have a talk without delay. If you should leave without our seeing each other, a life of misery will await us both. . . . And think of it! Our misunderstanding can be disspelled with a single word! You saw, didn't you, by my reply (the long letter) that my feelings remain the same? What more can I say?

Undated [1904].

My dear friend,

How many letters I have written and torn up! I have no faith in myself, and I have such a dread of being mistaken. . . .

Last evening I had intended to plead with you to let me see you both. I telephoned to you in the forenoon, but you were at the theatre. Then I waited for you—I had arranged to be free—but heard nothing from you. I thought you might have company, or that you were out.

I am *never* with our relatives. The men, who are most to blame for my being separated from my child and my wife, I do not care to know.
I am almost always alone—(with you!). . . .
If you do come, you will see no one but me!

. . . . . .

And so: I shall be waiting for you—I am waiting now. . .

Undated [1904].

At the moment of leave-taking—unavoidable as death—I envisioned all that was beautiful . . . and the most beautiful was my Sunday mornings this past winter. . . .
When I entered your home and saw you with our child at your breast, then I saw the loveliest I have seen in life: the mother and the child—and I think of these Sunday mornings as shining sunlight, illuminating the only happiness life bestows.
But it was not to remain so . . . Why? There is no answer!
Now the summer is approaching—the summer that we like to think of as the festive season of the year. If we three could only cling together, how the world would envy us. . . .
The little one gives me so much joy; yet always I am conscious of a shadow of sadness: she makes me think of the broken bond, of all that is missing. And whenever she is with me, she cries for her mother . . . and then I feel all the suffering that will come to her . . . and the disharmony from which she already is suffering. . . .
This week I am going out to the country, and I am now bidding you farewell! That our little child is welcome, you know; that she will be well taken care of by me, you know also; that she will breathe fresh, pure air in my home—where there is no guilt and where a clean conscience reigns—that you must know, too!
Do not meddle with the past but let the beauty of that final Sunday morning remain my last memory!

(Signed . . . with the name that you could never pronounce.)

Undated [1904].

The sufferings in store for us, beloved, will surpass anything we have undergone so far.

You are about to take an Inferno journey to Paris, torn by loneliness for the child—perhaps you will have to turn back—or you may take sick.

I am sitting with our little child, who is crying for her mother; and when I can't console her, she shows anger. She will not be able to bear this, and she will not eat at the same table with me, because you are not here.

There are moments when I think that she will become sick of living, and leave us. Her arrival brought us happiness, and she ennobled our union, gave us an interest in life. But she needs a home, and parents; she wants to have relatives and to see her parents closely united. It is only with us two that she is happy. And only when we three are together, do I see any light. We three: man, woman and child were a world to ourselves—justified, complete, sufficient to ourselves, and therefore beautiful. When we three drove about at midday of a Sunday, the crowds bowed their heads in respect, and we would not even have had to take a backseat to royalty, if we had not cared to and had not found it proper. And now we are parting! Do you see any real reason for it?

I do not! I did not leave you! I have been sitting waiting—and am still waiting!

You have been away seeking happiness in your freedom from me . . . Have you found it? Do you think happiness is found unalloyed, or that it can be bought? It can be gained through suffering and sacrifice—and then it can be so intense that one can be sustained by the memory of it for years to come.

The memory of one Sunday morning still keeps me alive. . . .

> I went to France with a girl friend. Both she and I were depressed and were trying to suppress our bitter memories by enjoying to the utmost all that Paris has to offer in the way of art and beauty.

Although I longed for Strindberg, I realized that we could never again share a home together. It went against my nature to be caged in. Everything within me, my high spirits and my curiosity about life, rebelled against this moribund existence. I had to choose whether to continue my career in the theatre or to close my eyes and ears to the world outside and wall myself up with Strindberg. My conscience was torn night and day, for though I loved Strindberg I also loved my personal freedom. I tried to silence all these doubts and mental inquisitions that forced themselves upon me, by whatever distractions I could find. In Paris I received the following letter from Strindberg. Our little daughter was staying with her father at Furusund in the Stockholm archipelago.

[4–6 June, 1904.]

Saturday, 4 June: Axel here. Beethoven night.

Sunday, 5 June: Our little one, who received uncle Axel at the steamboat landing, escorted him home and conversed with him. He succumbed to her immediately. We go for walks—we three—and Lillan keeps our spirit and us alive—we, who have lost our anchor in life.

In the afternoon, thunder and rain, followed by a rainbow. Axel returned [to Stockholm] in the evening.

Monday, 6 June: Just received two post cards from you this evening, Harriet.

Are we now separated? I have absolutely no information! Never mind—let us continue to write until further notice. . . .

You are in Paris—and I have had you in my room all the livelong day . . . Evidently there are no distances between us. And so we can't be ordinary mortals, can we? That thought has exalted me, and I am trying to adjust my life accordingly. I feel it my calling to persuade humanity that the world we live in is not the best, and that another world, a better one, is awaiting us. It is a gospel of hope, and that is my doctrine. In gratitude they strike me in the face, the fools. And this has been my teaching throughout my writings, not least in my latest work.

Your child is well-behaved and good. She twitters all the day long—never cries—lies awake without complaining. We are so attached to each other that I dread the moment when we must part, for she will miss me.

Sister Philp is living here (on the island) but I do not wish to resume any social intercourse until I am certain that I am quite alone in life; until then I will not admit any strangers into our little one's home . . . where your spirit is still present. I shall fill the void subsequently.

The swallows are nesting in our cottage. The first evening, they stayed on the hillside, trying to find out what kind of creatures we were. When they learned that we were neither ugly nor evil, they moved in.

Beethoven has consecrated the house, which in the beginning was a trifle recalcitrant.

Greta is arriving here to act at the Furusund Theatre with a Finnish travelling company.

Peace reigns in the house, and our little one is being watched over carefully. . . .

Take care of yourself!

August Strindberg

[9 June, 1904.]

Now I am doing as I did on Karlavägen: I am adorning the home in homage to your spirit. I know it visits here—at least our child! And I think that your spirit can feel whether it is lovely here or not. In order to make her feel at home, I had the large room decorated in your favorite color, the faintest shade of violet, with three narcissus blossoms. I also put up new curtains, designed with flowers and birds and of a texture as delicate as a dream. And if you should come here for a stay, be it brief or long, I have a room one flight up that is as friendly, as private and quiet as a bird's nest. And there I would make a bed on the floor—a brother and sister bed—out of our two mattresses, which have finally come together out here after such a long separation. I would sew the two together with silken thread, and I would sew our coverlets into one, and the sheets, too. Then I would sleep upon your arm, and you on mine—and in each other's arms . . . if you would come . . . But I have heard nothing! Have asked Millar by letter, but he does not answer. We live on a little island, green, bright, by the open sea, so that one can hear the plash while lying in bed. We are living, literally, in a bed of primroses and orchids.

Lillan is in good humor, never cries, is gentle and caressing. When life is hard on her, she smiles and engages me in conversation; and her warm, soft little hand guides me over the rocks a few steps forward. She seems to be on good terms with life and to have no fear of the frightening human creatures. She makes acquaintances by herself, preferably with grown-ups. The apothecary is her good friend, and the other day she introduced herself to a German. Sigrid was unable to determine what language they spoke.

I am now reading Emerson, whom Maeterlinck so frequently refers to as his teacher. I am also reading Novalis, who seems to hail from the same regions as Maeterlinck. So I am not lonely. Consorting with spirits (in the books)—my relatives. Emerson has satisfactorily explained Swedenborg to me. He has shown me how great he is.

Yesterday I received from Schering *Das Theater,* in which he has written about "Strindberg's Dream Stage," illustrated by two scenes from *To Damascus.*

Send me for once a kind letter. . . .

Hatred is vain and impotent, while kindliness and good will are all powerful! If people would only realize that!

Sunday morning, 12 June, 1904.
Harriet,

Thanks for your friendly post card with greetings from Orfila and Mme. Charlotte's! But did you see my rainbow on the dyer's glass door in Rue de Fleurus, to the left of the Luxembourg Garden?

The bow in the sky = No more deluge!

Great hubbub! Our child was stung by a mosquito! The naughty insect! Uncle Axel and uncle Svennberg here. Beethoven evening—until I dozed off with the sun in my face.

Noticed Antoine's repertory for next season: *King Lear*, adapted by Pierre Loti (the little lieutenant!), *Old Heidelberg*, etc. No Maeterlinck!

How will this summer end? Everything so uncertain, confused, threatening! Have you arrived at a clear conclusion yet?

Gusten

[Letter to Stockholm]

18 June, 1904.

Beloved,

I bid you welcome and would have expressed my joy over your last letter, but my answer would not have reached you in Paris.

I have built two cabins for us, close to each other; i.e., I have put in order two small, adjoining rooms, so that if you wish to have our little child to yourself, all you have to do is to close the door, which of course you may open whenever you feel like it. It is on the lower floor, where after all it is more comfortable. If you wish to change, you have merely to say so. But wait until you see it!

And we have an excellent piano for ourselves. Mail, newspapers, and the best in reading matter are delivered to us every evening. I have brought Emerson (whom Maeterlinck has translated) with me.

I have not visited the barroom here, and do not intend to; but may go to the bowling alley with you.

Our little one has had a stomach ache, but Sigrid helped her with massage. The result was instantaneous, and now she is well again. We have changed her diet. . . .

And now: with my arms wide open to you—welcome, my dearest.

Your

Gusten

After my visit in France I returned again to Sweden—to Furusund, where I had promised Strindberg to come and visit for a few weeks. He had, as usual, arranged things beautifully for me; he had given me the best room, had put everything in order and had fussed in every way to make me feel at home. I remember this summer as the quietest period of our marriage. Strindberg always loved little Anne-Marie dearly. She was now two years old and was able to walk about and to chat with him. He beamed with joy when she became timid or frightened; he then would pick her up joyfully, glad for the opportunity to hold her in his arms.

He could not do enough for his Anne-Marie. He fulfilled her slightest wish. But one time—when we were out walking at Furusund—Anne-Marie caught sight of a couple of puppies playing in a backyard. Strindberg detested dogs. I noticed how he stood holding little Anne-Marie in his arms, struggling with himself. "You know I don't wish to deny her anything—you know that—but I just cannot give her a dog!" And with this he turned abruptly and walked away. He was afraid he might succumb to the temptation to give her a puppy dog.

During his stay at Furusund Strindberg wrote a considerable part of *Play on Words and Art in Miniature*. The preceding summer (1903) he wrote his *Fairy Tales* for Anne-Marie.

These works of his were given to me to read little by little as they progressed. All the plays, too, that he wrote during our marriage, he also asked me to read, act by act, as they were being written.

From Furusund I travelled direct to Helsingfors [Helsinki], where I appeared as a guest artist in 1904. Strindberg returned to Stockholm with Anne-Marie.

In Helsingfors I received the following letter from him.

29 August, 1904.
Report no. 1.

Dear friend,

Our little Anne-Marie is again in her bright golden room, where she first saw the light of day. She officiated last evening as hostess, presiding on Mamma's throne chair until eight o'clock, while uncle Axel and aunt Anna played the Kreutzer Sonata (violin and piano).

During the night she frightened us when she suddenly developed mild cramps in her stomach, and she was uneasy in Mamma's bed because it was too wide for her. Finally she ended up sleeping with Ellen, which I didn't know until morning. She was then a little palenosed; but she ate her egg, drank her milk and behaved quietly. The whole thing was merely a sanitary process—for when Inez telephoned, we learned that she had consumed two oranges and one pear the day before yesterday—not to mention the strawberries she ate. Anne-Marie was impregnated with the intelligence that fruit is dangerous to eat during the fall season. In return, this question from her: "When, then, should one eat fruit? During the winter and the summer, when there is no fruit? When shall one eat it, then, if not in the fall, when there *is* fruit?" *C'est la vie quoi!*

However: Our child slept on the sofa in my study. It was one o'clock. Sister Anna came and played Godard. Inez came—Lillan was still asleep. I invited the oldsters (forgive the expression) to have some wine, and they actually fraternized!

It is evening now . . . you are about . . . I can sense you!

Our child is sleeping—there is silence everywhere!

I can't say it is agreeable—but it is nice to have the child here and to have someone to fuss over. The moment I turn her over to somebody else's care, she cries for her Mamma! Such moments are not so pleasant!

All good to you!

Your friend

Post card dated 31 August, 1904.

Thank you for your kind letter!

The little one is well again. I am remaining until further notice on Karlavägen—waiting for the next gust of wind.

Nothing is happening!

In friendship

A.S.

1 September, 1904.

Dear friend,

I have sent you a letter and a post card; and I have written two letters which I have not posted.

I can't write to you, as I speak with you all the day long in my thoughts and I feel that you already know everything—and a letter can be so dull!

Our little child is in good health, but has been sick. She has been drooping in my arms like a broken flower—it made me sad.

You have no doubt felt this when your spirits were low. It is so hard for me to deny our child anything which is not good for her; and when I am severe, and she cries, I suffer indescribably. I always think of how terribly I would reproach myself for this and that, if she should pass away.

Lillan has had her own little bed returned here and now feels more at home. But she is not happy. I think she misses you; but she is silent and only broods. The afternoons she spends at the big sand pile down below; the forenoons with aunt Inez.

I am sitting here waiting, prepared to accept as the best solution whatever may happen. Any solution will be difficult to bear . . . yet it is unavoidable—if it comes to pass.

Wish you well!

Your friend Nameless

I addressed this letter to the Swedish Theatre, Helsingfors.

2 September, 1904.

My dear friend,

In order to put an end to these eternal dissensions, let us loose the bonds which have come to mean nothing and are only oppressive. Then let us see what happens!

We need merely obtain an affidavit that we have been living apart from the fall of 1903 to the spring of 1904. Nothing irrelevant must be brought into the petition; and give careful thought to the fact that a certain similarity in our natures is neither your "fault" nor mine. And take care that you do not cast a shadow on our child's legitimacy. If you do, my in-

terest in her would be dead for all time. And the child would be in peril of martyrdom at school, and throughout life.
Therefore let Millar go ahead with the proceedings!
I hate this unnatural bond that makes my life dependent upon yours, puts my honor at the mercy of your behavior. But I do not hate you, and would like us to part as friends.
We can't have any more children, for we must be free in order to grow in our art!
This is my profoundest and my last desire!
Your friend
August Strindberg

5 September, 1904.
Having promised to write about our child, I shall do so.
Yesterday—Sunday, September 4th—Lillan had her great day. In the morning she and I drove alone in a carriage to Rosendal and looked at the flowers and the sunshine.

At eleven Inez and Alf came to fetch the much sought after child and they went away.

Between one and three o'clock she slept—in her own bed which she had had returned to her [from the country]. At three she was awakened by aunt Anna, cousin Märtha and uncle Hugo Fröding, whose Svea Life Guard uniform she has fallen in love with. (He is now serving the final year of his conscription term.) And then she was escorted to table by cousin Märtha, attracting general admiration for her fine manners and her beautiful eyes.

After dinner the engaged couple occupied the "sweetheart" sofa in Papa's study. Aunt Anna played Godard, and little Anne-Marie acted out several roguish comedy scenes, most of them tricks intended to disturb the two lovers in the sofa.

At five uncle Axel arrived, inviting us to take a drive with him, and Papa ordered a second carriage.

Uncle Axel, aunt Anna, Ellen, Nancy and Lillan took place in one carriage, and the lovers and Papa in the other. Then the parade to Djurgården and Liding Isle Bridge commenced.
It was fun!

At Liding Isle Bridge we took a walk on the bridge in the

lovely sunset, skipped stones across the water, dug in the sand—and then we drove the little one home beneath the stars. When she was going to bed all the relatives paid their homage to her. Twice they came in to say goodnight. . . . Lillan's Sunday was a bright one—only Mamma was missed. Poor Mamma!

Picture post card.
15 October, 1904.
[Postmark of that date]

To my beloved Mamma,
Do not worry! I shall never forget you, never in eternity!
(By my own hand)
Anne-Marie

19 October, 1904.

Harriet,
I do not wish to disturb you, but do not tarry any longer than you have to. Lillan misses you, and the care that only a mother can give. She cries during the nights and wants to sleep with Nancy, who is kind to her, but—Nancy is a child herself.

Forget you? Can a child forget its mother? We all try to divert her. She likes me, but all others she tolerates according to the degree that they amuse her. She has a magnificent retinue—from the old Frödings and the young Frödings to a genuine, although young, navy captain, a young army volunteer, and several others. She is frequently invited to the Frödings, who are nice, good people, but they have recently suffered misfortunes—which, however, have now come to an end.

Ellen left—in anger, of course, as was to be expected—and for reasons unknown. Her successor is good-tempered, neat and tidy; the kitchen has been transformed into a beautiful room, where our Lillan feels at home at the table in the center. The table is covered by a cloth, and the servants take turns reading fairy tales to her by the lamp light.

Perhaps by this time the legal phase of our divorce has been completed. You have your freedom—and I have helped you to get it! Do you feel happy with it? Do you really feel free now?

Comparing the present with the autumn of three years ago, when I wept for forty days and forty nights, it seems to me as if the road were brighter, as if I could see the light. . . .

I cannot write . . . have worried so much about others. . . .

I have shared your suffering with you when you were low in spirit. . . . If you ever felt any joy, I do not know—but I hope you did!

Life seems to me so mockingly cruel. Only a cynic, it seems to me, could endure it!

I yearn to go to Switzerland, and I shall probably be away from this country for a long time. . . .

Return soon to your child, but do not worry: she becomes attached to no one, and can hardly tolerate any strangers in my house, which she feels is her home.

August Strindberg

After having concluded my guest appearances in Helsingfors I returned to Stockholm, where I had rented an apartment for myself and Anne-Marie. While in Finland I had missed her so very much, although I knew that she was well cared for while with her father.

The divorce had now gone into effect.
I parted from Strindberg during my season in Finland in 1904. Just as in the past, he visited us often, and our child and I continued to be his guest on Sunday afternoons.

An incident from one of our visits comes to my mind, showing what a sublime and lofty opinion of humanity Strindberg was eager to hold, and how he suffered when his expectations were shattered.

I had been at his home one Sunday and had been playing the piano for him. In order to play unhampered, I removed my ring—my engagement ring with brilliants and sapphires—given me by Strindberg. I placed the ring beside me on the piano. When I departed, I forgot to put it on again. On my return home, I telephoned to him and asked him to look for it and keep it for me. Strindberg replied that the ring was not there. A search for it throughout the apartment was of no avail. Several floor planks were removed, yet there was no sign of any ring.

At dinner on the following Sunday afternoon, I spoke about the mysterious disappearance of the ring, and the maid who waited on the table expressed her regrets in a manner I thought a trifle too effusive, so that I, quite intuitively, could not help but feel suspicious of her. I confided my suspicions to Strindberg. He lost his temper completely and exclaimed heatedly: "She could never have taken the ring! . . . She may be poor, but she is an honest girl! It is a crime to think she has taken it

—merely because she holds a position that is considered inferior by society."

Six months after this incident, Strindberg's maid came to my home, asking to see me. He now had a different maid; the former one had left him. The new maid related to me that Strindberg had received a telephone call one day from a family, by whom the other maid was now employed, inquiring whether he had ever missed a ring, set with brilliants and sapphires. The lady had discovered such a ring on the maid's dresser, and —because of its value—she could not help but wonder whether it actually belonged to her. For that reason she had telephoned to Strindberg, knowing that the girl had been employed by him; and he had immediately recognized the ring by the description.

The new maid brought the ring with her, and she told me that when the telephone conversation was over, Strindberg had collapsed completely, crying like a little child. Strindberg left it to me to decide whether to hand over the girl to the police authorities or not. I could not bear to see her punished, and therefore refused to prosecute. I was, however, glad to have the ring returned.

By having my own apartment now, I seemed to regain my equilibrium. I was able to devote myself more assiduously, and in greater peace and quiet, to my duties at the theatre. Now and then I could not help but feel melancholy, however. I felt alone—I needed someone to talk to. I assume I must have mentioned this to Strindberg, for he wrote me as follows:

[19 December, 1904.]

Harriet,

Daily in my thoughts, and in the dreams of the night, I seem to feel that you are not happy—that humanity and the world bring you pain; and I feel as if you were seeking me often . . . Are you? If I can advise you, if I can console you, you know that I am with you whenever you call upon me—for I am as close to you as ever I was, both you and Lillan. No one has yet been able to take your place—you both.— I have the most beautiful of memories from your home on Biblioteksgatan.

Don't you feel that I am following you with my good will? "Wholeheartedly I wish you all that's good . . . yes, even though you left me."

5 P.M., 20 December, 1904.

Two hours ago I dispatched my letter, written yesterday, by Svea. Now I have just received yours—also written yesterday.

Your soul was troubled yesterday—I felt it.

What is wrong? Have you carelessly meddled with the fates of others so that they plague you with their hatred at a distance? It is dangerous to awaken powerful feelings without returning them. It is much like touching the accumulator in an electric powerhouse.

You are aware that a strong, evil spirit is pursuing you, aren't you, and that this demon is trying to keep us apart. But I believe that my affection protects you—while you are asleep and when you are awake. He has sworn to possess you —merely for the sake of possession, not out of love, for he does not know what love is. If necessary, he will steal your honor with lies, as others have done, or he will do away with you—in your sleep or by the light of day—with his hate.

I saw him in my dreams recently—he is inhuman. Beware of him!

. . . . . .

Do not tangle your fate with that of the first one you meet, by being unnecessarily intimate. There will always be a rent somewhere when you try to break loose. . . .

Feel that I am your support, that my kindly thoughts follow you wherever you go. Repeatedly during the day my goodwill and good thoughts go out to you. I pray for your comfort and for peace in your house . . . that your child will be kind to you, and your servant faithful and devoted. . . .

But what about Christmas?

[*December, 1904.*]

Harriet,

I am waiting! That is an art I have learned! But Christmas, the child's Christmas!

Do you think we have acted rightly, robbing her of her father? Do you think she realizes that the trinity has been disjointed? While her mother is closest to her, Papa and Mamma united were surely safer, more secure, more beautiful, more complete.

What kind of Christmas do you want? Last year we had a double one—this year none!

I am prepared for anything; and for the child's sake I am willing to be subjected to any and all humiliations.

What has happened to you today, Monday? Something hard to bear? You have been hovering about me as if you were pleading for help . . . Is our little one ill? Has anyone been unkind to you? I know who your enemies are—but I dare not warn you . . . you wouldn't trust me and my motives.

[*22 December, 1904.*]

And so

Into the faraway. . . .

So be it!

Here simply a few practical questions:

1. What does Lillan want for Christmas? She has been speaking about a rocking-horse.
2. I would like to give Alf something from our little one because he has given her pleasure. But what?
3. Lillan is expected for dinner Christmas Eve. Have you received the divorce papers? And the court's decision? May I see them, and copy?

[*December, 1904.*]

Dear friend,

I have bought the violin—and a real one—that a child can practice on. . . .

Chairs and tables, however, were sold out. As I did not dare choose anything else, I will ask you to purchase exactly what you want and send the bill to me. Will you do that?

What was wrong with you today? I have seen you in a mist all day long . . . I became uneasy about you—and just then Alf arrived.

Couldn't Alf come along to the dinner at my house on Christmas Eve—it would be a little livelier? Our little child and I are a trifle quiet, I am afraid. . . .

Our Lillan's aunt Elisabeth passed away at Uppsala Asylum a fortnight ago. This is how she looked,* the unfortunate one, who never knew a happy day in her life. She was like a twin sister to me, and when she died we offered thanks.

I only wish to show you the "Easter girl." She suffered for others, and took their sins upon herself. Therefore she could not be as kind as she might have been otherwise.

After our divorce in 1904 we each lived in our separate apartments. From then on I was never to share a home with Strindberg again. However, we continued to visit each other for some years following our separation; and his friendship and concern for me extended to the time of my second marriage.

In the letter below, Strindberg thanks me for his Christmas Eve at my home:

New Year's Day, 1905.

Beloved,

Must thank you for Christmas Eve, which I shall treasure as one of my loveliest memories . . . I beheld you in the surroundings that befit you: unique, sovereign, and adorned with a most precious jewel—the child!

And I saw the mother, undressing her child for the night. . . .

That is how I should like to picture your bedroom. . . .

You—so proud—wanted a man at your side! It was a mis-

* Strindberg enclosed her photograph in the letter.

take, which has now been corrected! But it was for the sake of the child! Indeed, I feel myself honored!

. . . . . .

The reunion seemed natural to me—but I sensed a strange and hostile world behind you, and it frightened me. Curious that you, moving among my enemies, can harbor friendly feelings toward me. But I presume it is this inconsistency that is at the core of love's nature, of genuinely great love—"despite everything"!

The visible bond could be broken, but the invisible one was indestructible! I seem to find it acceptable as it is; and from afar I visualize you as come from realms on high. I don't think we are real mortals—but that we come from a place somewhat higher and have been cast deep down here: that is why we ever struggle within our bodies and why we are unhappy and ill at ease. . . .

Last night at twelve I felt your fragrance leap up like a sharp outcry, which I gave answer to!

Wonder sometimes whether there is some little soul longing to have us as parents again, driving us together. . . .

2 January, 1905.

My friend,

You are right: what is hidden in the heart should not be profaned by the gaze of mortals . . . That is why I always refused to allow ourselves to be exhibited.

Tomorrow, Sunday, you are free the whole day, and—however much I shall miss Lillan—we must try to have a talk quite by ourselves. I am sending Ebba to the theatre tomorrow evening, in order that we may be absolutely undisturbed here the whole evening.

But if you and Lillan care to have dinner with me here, then Ellen wouldn't have to do any cooking and dishwashing; and she would be sure to watch with still greater care over your home in the evening.

Let me know your desire!

For the rest, you may come and go in my home, as you please. I am alone most of the time.

Your friend
"Strindberg"

During the summer of 1905 I went to Hornbaek in Denmark with my little girl. Of Hornbaek I had many memories. I found it beautiful when I spent the summer there during the first year of our marriage. Strindberg, on the other hand, went out to Furusund in the Stockholm skerries. He had longed to get away from the city; and this summer he had rented a different cottage from the one we had occupied in 1904.

[Letter to Hornbaek]

Sunday morning, 18 June, 1905.
Dear friend,
I have been wondering how things are with you. I have sensed you so powerfully every day, yesterday (Saturday) especially. Was afraid that Lillan was sick.

I, too, can picture the loveliness from here, much like a memory of youth: the "first love"—the wedding trip . . . and it seemed to me, from the hell in which I found myself, that every time I saw Mölle on the opposite side, and Helsingborg, and the cathedral in Lund, the sight of them appeared like a dream of Paradise. I imagined myself on "the other side," with the Sound being the River of Death—and thought I had entered Paradise . . . yet, alas, outside stood the dreaded house with the gallows on the roof and my friend Philipot from my Inferno days in Lund.

Our little one has been at Hornbaek before—when she was no bigger than a cherry—and her cradle, the first one she had, was the waves . . . outside the bath house—in her mother's lap. . . .

It is not surprising that she feels thoroughly at home and is happy!

Perhaps it is a grace to forget—for only by forgetting the past can we gain the future!

You may already—since you wrote your letter—have left behind the old? But if you continue to feel ill at ease in your surroundings, say but one word and I shall dispatch the help!

. . . . .

I hardly think I can endure the city! "Long, tedious, dreary evenings!"

This morning the dining table collapsed without warning. A wood block fell off where you and I usually sit! What can this mean?

Rely on me! You know that I both can and wish to help, and I am not miserly. . . .

[7 July, 1905.]

Harriet,

If I should again be mistaken in my feelings, I have to run that risk. . . .

Where are you? Are you happy? Have you left behind the past? Are you unhappy? Shall I help you?

I am at our honeymoon island! The loveliest, most unspoiled and most peaceful spot I ever knew. Like a sea gull's nest . . . a place where one can hide. . . .

Prosperous and affluent—but without happiness!

Anyone who cannot enjoy good fortune by himself alone cannot be such an egoist as people like to think!

If you seek an escape from people, this is the place to secrete yourself! Here you have the open sea, cottages and people—but no one bothers you!

Send me a word by telegraph if you long for the north. . . .

Täckholmen is inviting as a wide open pair of arms, and friendly! We were in error about the place.

23 July, 1905.
[Date of the postmark.]

Harriet,

The summer is over, thus . . . Next Saturday I am moving back [to the city].

I don't wish to make you feel unhappy, but within the past five days I have read four times of children being kidnapped! I have been worrying ever since, and must warn you! Don't ever leave our little child alone, and caution Ellen! . . .

· · · · · ·

Now I have done my duty!
If I at least could age sufficiently swiftly and become resigned! But I have put on weight, have turned red and brown!
But baffled expectations make the heart sick. Loneliness forces one to seek out others.

· · · · · ·

Afterward, the breaking up of the old household will commence.
And after that?
You will not have to travel third class coming back!
Thus: the summer is over. . . .

During my stay at Hornbaek plans for my appearance on the German stage again came to the fore. Strindberg was indefatigable in his efforts—he had often in the past suggested that I make an attempt to act in German—and he now advised that I actually carry the plan into effect. But he cautioned me against acting in his plays in Germany. He was afraid that it might be detrimental to my career to make my first appearance there in his sombre dramas.

[Letter to Hornbaek]

29 July, 1905.*

My dear friend,
I cannot advise you. But I am afraid of Vienna and the Strauss waltzes. Especially if you are thinking of doing *Easter*. No—not that!—Later on—in Berlin. But it is so difficult to

* Strindberg had dated this letter 28 July, 1905, by mistake.

judge!—Wait for some sign, or an inner urge! Schering is being guided by his own interests, frequently wrongly! Postpone, but do not say no!

. . . . . .

Am tired—so I'll say goodnight!

Sunday, 30 July, 1905.

Dear You,

Having slept on the matter, your Vienna journey now seems to me somewhat premature. But the offer can be an incentive to learn the German language gradually during the year.

My conflict in opinion stems from my inability to patch together my past viewpoints and my present one. New editions [of my works] and German retranslations . . . I hurl defiance at myself, unfetter spirits I once invoked, and—like Heine, I feel myself wanting. It is difficult to treat myself as two persons.

Last Thursday I was invited to the Svennbergs. I had not expected to find such an inviting, attractive home, with a Japanese garden park in the rear.

[Strindberg then gives a sympathetic description of Mrs. Svennberg and her sister.]

Yesterday, Saturday, they spent the evening with me. I valued (as you know that I do!) the company of the ladies, for it neutralizes male crudity and creates an urge to suppress, yes, what we call bad instincts. One shows the best within oneself in order to give the most favorable impression—as for a festal occasion.

The atmosphere that of a family group, cultivated, reserved. In brief, delightful! . . . .

The day after tomorrow I shall leave here—August 1.

Let me know when you are leaving your domicile, and then I shall send you some money for travelling—second-class—100 crowns.

Keep our little one away from that lady with the cane! She is not from the Danube, is she?
Did you read that the gypsies down there have devoured children? Cannibals!
Thunder and rain every day—raining this very moment. . . .
Address Karlavägen from now on!

> Strindberg repeatedly invited me to come out to Furusund with our little daughter and to be his guest there that summer. This never came about, however. It seemed as if the bond could never be broken, and I suffered from it. Thus I tried to remain in Denmark. Had he shown anger, or flared out against me, it would have been so much easier to forget. But he was always so kind and helpful—and that is why I could not help but feel attached to him.

4 August, 1905.
[The date of the postmark]

. . . . . .

Now as to your letter! Yes, dear child, loneliness is a punishment—and one says whatever may come to mind . . . and one becomes bizarre, too.
We quarrel by mail like old married people!
You are not asking me to live in absolute loneliness, are you, when you yourself don't do it?
Here it is so beautiful, rainy and cold!

10 August, 1905.
[The date of the postmark]

Dear child,
You will be well again when you return to your home in Sweden; and when you appear behind the footlights you will be your own self again.
And when you both are here, we can discuss a home for

our child during your absence. She must not be left alone with E—n [Ellen], for she beats her, when she loses her temper. I shall no doubt be able to find a home, where I can keep an eye on her . . . while you are in Finland.

Pay no attention to my last letter. I have heard nothing from the Danube as yet.

Seven more days, then!

In friendship.

In the autumn of 1905 I was engaged to appear as a guest artist at the Grand Theatre in Gothenburg. A most interesting and promising repertory had been arranged for the season. I looked forward to having an opportunity to act in a play by Maeterlinck, whom I admired. During the preceding season the plays in which I had acted, had proved to be rather insipid, and they had dulled my interest in my work. Now—with the prospect of appearing in excellent plays—my ardor returned; and I anticipated joyfully my engagement at the Gothenburg theatre.

However, the season commenced with ancient fare, and it appeared as if the rehearsals for Maeterlinck's *Pelléas and Mélisande* were being deferred indefinitely.

Letter to Gothenburg

13 September, 1905.

Dear friend,

All is well on board; nothing has happened. . . . . But why are you not rehearsing? I do not understand the situation. It seems muddled!

My work (The History of Sweden, told in story form) is a heavy task; but it has to be written for the sake of house and home. The presence of Anne-Marie is a source of brightness, but the absence of "the third party" brings sadness to the heart. Our child is no longer a baby; therefore I am beginning to feel superfluous—feel myself detached from life and its interests . . . am losing the incentive to be part of the world and of life, and long to leave it. To hover about and above what remains of life . . . to be ready to set sail whenever summoned. . . .

In the Sirishov Bay . . . a white canoe has drifted ashore . . . I wonder whether it is waiting for me—has come to take me away!. . . .

I am ready to depart—my whole life has been one long preparation for that journey!

Your
August Sg.

16 September, 1905.

Dear child,

It brightened! If one now should ask: Why didn't you open with . . . ?—then fourteen days of anguish would not have been suffered in vain. To this I answer myself, as you well know: C'est plus fort que moi . . . And I console myself—as you also know—with this thought: It was inevitable—it had to be . . . But Who forced me to torture myself? Don't know. It was someone not myself—someone with a definite intent—and in the end it was discovered that the intention was good.

Of this Someone, I know only that He rules my fate, and ever leads me to the goal, although circuitously. This was what you found so difficult to grasp when we set out together and you still believed that we humans were the masters of our fate! It often agonized me that I could not convince you. . . .

When you tell me about your room and its inconveniences —that others fail to see—what comes to your mind, then? To you it is all a definite and obvious actuality; and you could point it out to others. Therefore this is no hallucination. . . .

Theosophists would say that it is either the unclean thoughts of strangers or your own thoughts, projecting themselves. . . .

I believe in witchcraft and sorcery, as you know . . . Perhaps they are warnings from our invisible Masters. . . .

I cannot explain some things in a natural way . . . But one should not discuss such things with everyone.

Yes—the world is full of wonders. . . .

Your friend
August Sg.

17 *September, 1905.*
Sunday evening.

Dear friend,

Anne-Marie is sleeping, the Stranger on the first floor is playing E minor, Rosa sits forgotten on my sofa, her eyes wide open, and dressed in rosy red (Rosa was presented last evening to Henning Berger who came in for a little while). We had a whisky and soda. The house is silent; both Ebba and Sarah are quiet and unobtrusive. . . .

I have been in a kind of blessed state of ecstacy and rapture all day—as if I had met with some strange happiness. I have now emerged from the coalmines of my Swedish History; feel that I am again back in the present—which is the best of all times, for everything that is past is compost nourishing the roots of the present.

What is now to come? The beautiful present is my answer. . . .

My book * will not be published before October 1st, but it will be an exceptionally handsome volume to look at.

Eysoldt has been touring with *Miss Julie* in Switzerland. She will also play the rôle in Berlin in the fall—with Reinhardt at the Deutsches Theater.

Goodnight!

28 September, 1905.

My dear friend,

If you feel that you are being injured soul and body by this Inferno journey, then save yourself before you have become completely fettered.

. . . .

* Strindberg no doubt refers to *Historical Miniatures*, published in 1905.

Your fate, now hovering like a cloud, drifts all the way to this apartment. I am oppressed by it, sharing your uneasiness and your hopes. Why can't one escape this? Is it inevitable?

The contact with human beings—hopeless, disconsolate, anguished—has pulled me down . . . and I am struggling again to free myself and go upward!

Goethe's *Tasso* is a help to me; it has wisdom and throws light on certain obscure matters. . . .

And besides it is autumn: no sun—heavy and burdensome . . . and my thoughts are anchored in oppressive Gothenburg, in the wretched Göta Källare where I have been through an Inferno three different times!

Your friend
August Sg.

1 October, 1905.

Dear friend,

And now I must congratulate you! It is forever like struggling with demons. If one wins, it is by a miracle.

Anne-Marie is now a big girl. She is teaching me how to speak the Swedish language.

"Papa must not say 'y-e-e-s' but 'yes'." She has also informed me that I have green hair.

She yearns for her mother to come and play with her and to hold her hand at night.

At this moment she is visiting the kindhearted Gustaf Janson, playing with his two little sons, whose acquaintance she made in the stairway.

She has also met one little Hervor, the three-year old daughter of a captain Lindström of the 1st Svea Army Corps, who lives here in this street.

Your daughter behaves nicely and is obedient; I never hear any screaming from her side of the corridor. But she has no love for porridge. However, as she is in good health and must eat, she is given other food. But she is not permitted to ravage the smörgåsbord.

The Dance of Death is now being presented in Germany

and is said to be a success. From Cologne it is going to Leipzig and Berlin, etc.

. . . . .

How long will you remain in Gothenburg?
Your friend
August Sg.

2 October, 1905.

My beloved,

Are you still writing to me, now that you have reached the heights and are idolized and worshiped! I am afraid I have lived in a sort of *Seconda Primavera* these last few days—perhaps because of the resurrection of *Easter*, which prompted thoughts of our engagement and marriage. As a result I was caught by a longing to redecorate your green room. I tore down the gauze from Blid Island, and behold—beneath was the green silk, fresh, protected from the dust of the past years. And now your dainty mahogany suite is again greening in the autumn . . . Let us today put on our rings—and then everything will be as of old!

What you say about Anne-Marie I have been afraid of. Therefore, if you plan to stay yet another month, wouldn't you like to have her with you in a *pension*?

She is developing so fast—not as a child, but as a young lady—that she frightens me. And since she is not conscious of any coercion, she forgets that she is a child—which she, in her mother's presence, would always be reminded of . . . I cannot be severe with her, cannot correct her because she has grown beyond me . . . She brings home to me new lessons, corrects me—precociously, humorously. She is most of the time outdoors and in the kitchen . . . she will be a stranger to us both. . . .

This may be the way of the world and cannot be prevented —but it can't help but make an impression.

Whatever you do, think of yourself now, so that the fruits of your victory are not lost!

Take no medicine for your cough, but take a strong drink before going to bed (warm *punsch*).

Must all beginning be hard? Must we be robbed of courage first? Is it always so, or only for us, we Königskinder?

Schering keeps sending telegrams giving news of the progress of *The Dance of Death* as it goes forward—much like an epidemic of cholera—on its tour [of Germany].

This morning another white boat lay stranded in the Sirishov Bay. It was an unmanned wreck, somewhat battered, and had two pair of oars with red blades. Also cast ashore were two buckets: one of blue paint, the other of red. "Faith and Charity!"

Your
August Sg.

Papa is only talking nonsense. Lillan loves her Mother and longs for her! Kisses!

Anne-Marie.

4 October, 1905.
[The date of the postmark]

Dearly beloved,

I feel that I have pained you with my last letter, but I could not help it. . . .

My discordant emotions tear me apart; my loneliness drives me to seek people out, but each time—even after a most genial contact—I withdraw injured and hurt and find myself still more depressed. I feel ashamed for no reason whatever, suffer remorse without having committed any wrong, loathe myself without knowing why. . . .

Today I have an urge to remove myself from life . . . I feel I have fulfilled my obscure mission . . . fear that I shall sink down into treacherous marshlands if I remain here . . . feel that a better home stands waiting for me somewhere far in the beyond. . . .

I can't help thinking of your dream the last day you were here: that I had died by my own hand. . . .

I fear that is what it will lead to, eventually, though I do not know why. I am striving toward the heights—but am sinking into the mire; I desire to do the right thing—yet act wrongly; my old self is at odds with my newborn personality: I yearn to discover beauty in life—but find beauty only in nature; I feel compassion for people—but cannot respect them—cannot love them. . . for I know them through myself. The only consolation given me, I receive from Buddha, who tells me quite frankly that life is a phantasm, an illusion, which we will only see in its right perspective in another life. My hope and my future lie on the other side—that is why I find life so hard to bear. Everything crumbles, every effort is spurned, turning into a mockery. Everything has to be viewed from afar. This morning I watched the vista from my writing desk . . . You know what an unearthly beauty it takes on in the sunlight . . . I was in ecstasy. When I went below to get a closer look from the field—the view disappeared behind the hilltops; and as I went toward it, all its beauty vanished! What one deliberately seeks, escapes one!

The wife, the child, the home were best. A hard school—but the only protection against evil influences. Without this protection I shall falter and go astray, shall fall victim of whoever may cross my path. Loneliness is not to be despised, but there again I am the prey of self-inflicted punishment, scourging myself sternly, mercilessly. . . .

Think of me with kindness—it will help me!

It is now four years since you returned with our little unborn child! I think of it now with gratitude, and a feeling of loss. . . .

Yours

6 October, 1905.

Dear You,

Thank you again for your friendly letter. My sadness has no special cause; it was merely an expression of my periodic feeling: the pain of existence—heavier, perhaps, in the fall.

Theosophy is not dangerous: It is the beautiful teachings of Buddha, which you learned to know in the Indian dramas, but which have now been changed into a theology, crammed with dogmas. It merits to be studied, though more severely narrow in outlook and more inexorable than Christianity, which can forgive without revenge—without entering in a ledger all the faults and stupidities we commit (the thief on the cross!).

If *Pelléas and Mélisande* succeeds beyond doubt, don't you think you ought to branch out and make a tour here, among other places?

I think this engagement has been a boon to you, after all. But how about your finances? If you have no money, I shall send you some—you must tell me if you need any.

The house is quiet, and all goes without fuss or bother. Mornings I greet your daughter with a coffee twist, which she awaits patiently, without any prodding. Evenings we have Great Meyer * and the drawing set—and then goodnight. She sleeps the night through without waking.

Let me now hear something about your repertory, how things are going, when the première takes place, etc.

Your friend
August Sg.

7 October, 1905.
My dear friend,

You have received still another offer from Schering; and I merely want to say that I have no part in it. I can guess what your answer will be!

Lillan is so delighted with her box, whose treasures seem inexhaustible; she sends a thousand thanks. I have now discovered a way to make her laugh: I speak Danish! . . .

Gyllensköld appeared on the scene last evening. He intended to travel to Gothenburg, when he heard that *Pelléas* was to be given there. I was almost tempted to join him, but—geht nicht!

Here we have had blackening rain for the last three weeks, and my spirit has been darkened, too. But the child is just as cheerful as ever—her hair as golden—and she grows more beautiful with every day that passes.

* *Meyer's Encyclopedia.*

Today I have been longing for Switzerland. . . .
It is now evening. Goodnight, my dear friend!
> Your
>
> August Sg.

> 16 October, 1905.
> [The date of the postmark]

Dear child,
Why Sarah is leaving? Because she wants to become a nurse . . . Why I am letting her go? Because she never plays with Lillan, and probably neither washes nor combs her. Lillan kept nagging her to give her a bath (and was given one). No doubt she felt she was in need of one. Besides, Sarah is a secretive person whom I am afraid of. I never know where she takes Lillan, having no way of controlling her movements . . . An occasional word from Anne-Marie indicates something I feel incapable of delving in.

She is now leaving on the 25th. She seems to have obtained a position. . . .

Was thun? Take an old woman, who knows how to bring up children?

Is there a possibility of your acting in *Easter* and *Pelléas* in Gothenburg. . . . ?

One detail: Will you dress [as Eleonora] in *Easter* as you did as Hedvig [in *The Wild Duck*]? It would help you!

. . . . . .

Do not go to Vienna on the spur of the moment . . . Wassermann has described Vienna in *Moloch!*

As for the program: Create *Easter* and *Pelléas*. Come home and make arrangements for Lillan. Return later—or go on tour, with a safe guarantee!

I am tired and in bad spirits, I also! And I feel my responsibility to Lillan, whom I can't protect from outside influences since I have no right to decide with whom she is to associate. She is gentle, well-behaved, and grateful when she is with me—

but the moment she has been out, she is a different child . . . You yourself anticipated the dangers of her being fondled and idolized.

Courage—for the last time! Soon it will be over!

Your
August Sg.

17 October, 1905.

My dear friend,

Your daughter gave a dinner party today for Hervor in the yellow room; and is accompanying Papa to Eldh's studio on Narvavägen, where I am sitting for a bust.

Last evening all the Beethoven cronies—including Bergh, Nordström, Gyllon [Gyllensköld] and Axel, even Carl Larsson. Uncle Larsson wants to paint Lillan next week; Bergh is painting Papa.

Vergiftet sind meine Lieder, wie könnte es anders sein! says Heine.

Yes, my dear, the bitter fruits of our discord and dissensions are now here. The moment which I had looked forward to with joy, when I could have dedicated my poems to you, has been turned into mortification. The fruits of last autumn were gall nuts—and when I wanted to expunge them, it was too late (already printed)!

This I have to let you know in time—or you would consider me false! I prefer to be frank—with its consequences . . . I am not to blame!

Was this your dream in August—recently!

But there will be another, a new edition, purified through suffering. This I shall dedicate to you, if our bond still holds!

Do not poke in the ashes! We will soon have burned so much refuse together, we two . . . let the ashes be! And let another day bring fresh experiences!

Your
August Sg.

18 October, 1905.

My dearest friend,
Of course I can keep going with Lillan! You know she is a dear little one to have around, and she gives me nothing but joy, mixed with a feeling of uneasiness for her. . . .
And soon you will be here again, and will feel that you are welcome among, perhaps, your only friends. And then you will look back upon these horrible months, as in a dream, in comparison with which the barren reality here nevertheless will make you feel at home. . . .
May *Pelléas* be a success, so that you can play it here!
The Gothenburgers seem to have superb taste, as the trash was not accepted, while *Juliet*, on the other hand, was a success. . . . Perhaps Castegren underestimates the theatregoers!
And now: Just a few more steps—and you will have arrived!
Your friend
August Sg.

20 October, 1905.

Beloved friend,
Let me now thank you for *Easter*—our *Easter!*
Too much social intercourse has brought on a feeling of disgust with the world, and I want to cry out: Now I am sinking . . . I miss the protecting family influence; even though it is a strain, it does not pull me down.
The mere contact with people wounds me! Yet we do them no harm. . . .
Lillan is thriving and never cries. She writes long letters to Mamma every day, and puts old stamps on them and hands them to Ebba. No doubt she thinks they are forwarded by the post office. The many "uncles" she has met, interest her, and she knows them all by name. Hugo Fröding, however, with his shining uniform buttons, is closest to her heart.
Now we are only waiting for Mamma to return; and soon you will be coming back with the golden fleece—even though it was hard to capture!
And now—welcome, dear little Mamma. . . .

Do you think Castegren will pay me my royalties? I am counting on them!
When will *Pelléas* be given?

22 October, 1905.

Beloved,
Yes, I was alone and with you in the apartment last Friday evening—this apartment that tolerates no one but us . . . It darkens and wrinkles its brow to strange men; and it is this company of men exclusively that is pulling me down. You will recall my innocent observation last summer—how the presence of a woman tends to elevate men. In her nearness, they not only show their better side but actually prove themselves to be better. And it is the dream of every man to seek salvation through a woman—salvation from all that is low and base.

Aloneness—but aloneness within the family, with its natural companionship: the relatives . . . that is how I imagined the comparative bliss that life has to offer.

It is possible, however, that women—when they are by themselves—do not display the same high qualities that they do in the presence of men . . . for the same reasons!

In a gathering of men I sometimes make an attempt to put a stop to a conversation by a sudden, well-timed silence. But it generally ends by the majority's holding the upper hand—and I am drawn down where I am loath to go—into the realm of coarseness and baseness . . . While—with but one to contend with—I usually get the upper hand. . . .

Now we have met again—with the Easter lily, the rod,* and *Swanwhite*, which all belong together in my memory of spring from Banérgatan and Grev-Magnigatan.

But what a long, long, roundabout way. . . .

Lillan and I are now counting the days . . . She says three, five, ten days—and then Mamma will be here! Indeed, she has not forgotten you—no, indeed!

You will see when you come!

* The Easter lily, the rod: Symbols of peace and penance.

Until then—and then: our embrace is wide open to you!
. . . .

from
Us Two

25 October, 1905.

Dear Heart!
I am as happy over the success of *Pelléas* as if it had happened to me myself.

Your
August Sg.

Over!

Elin has come. She looks able and honest, plain and good-natured.
Die Andere was mir zu schön—and she knew it!

27 October, 1905.

Dear friend,
Your child has bathed and now lies munching a pear, a picture of carefree abandon and well-being.

Uncle Larsson failed to come this time, but he will be back, and then Lillan is to be painted.

Uncle Bergh is painting Papa daily and will be ready in a few days.

It will be big in size and conception.

B.'s brother-in-law arrived from Gothenburg. He had been present at the Maeterlinck première and was enraptured over it.

The new Elin is excellent! Everything is as quiet as before, but better and more orderly and efficient.

And a week from tomorrow Mamma is back home again! That is the very best!

We
Papa and Lillan

28 October, 1905.

My dear friend,

Now that danger, too, is surmounted . . . the one with the *poems!*

And in a few days I can send them to you, poison free, after the publisher—for your sake—had disinfected the edition!

Your
August Sg.

29 October, 1905.

Dearest You,

Since you ask me, answer Ranft: "I shall appear with you as a guest artist in rôles chosen by myself!" Voilà tout!

Then you will get back your friends the Stockholmians! And be near your child!

Rich. B. tells me that Ranft is seriously reflecting on [producing] *The Crown Bride.*

Would you care to pull me out of my worries and undeserved oblivion by demanding the glorious rôle?

From Castegren I have received no royalties. He probably thinks I have no need of them—and I am reluctant to ask him.

Lillan and I are looking forward to seeing you next Saturday. She is counting on her fingers: five, seven, ten, eight days. And she has already composed the menu: flower buds with butter (crown artichokes), big crayfish (lobster); and Mamma is to sit in her great big chair—which no one has been permitted to occupy since she left.

Today Lillan is dining out: Elle dîne en ville (with Mrs. M.). She is very much taken with Papa's portrait; and uncle B. misses her little footsteps tripping into the dining-room, whenever she is not here. She always waits politely in the green room, and from there she asks: "May I come in?"— She never rushes in.

Elin is excellent, quick and reliable. She is ugly as sin, and therefore devoid of coquetry—which is especially agreeable to me!

Is *Pelléas* being given daily?

Do not remain too long in Gothenburg, so that all the plays lose drawing power before your benefit performance! * You must think of yourself first of all! And accept Ranft's proposal rather than going on tour with Castegren!

Thus: We shall see each other soon!

Your
August Sg.

31 October, 1905.

Dear You,

Is it wise to stay on after your benefit performance? When the culmination has been reached, there is nothing left but the decline.

No doubt you are surprised to hear that I need 150 crowns, after having recently offered to pay for your release [from the contract]. But the fact is that I—in order to help you—had intended to borrow the money, putting up the furniture as security.

Your daughter presided yesterday at the dinner table, with Richard B., and took charge of the service bell. "Shall we ring now?" said Bergh after the salmon (had been finished).

"I have not finished," said Lillan, cutting him off—and with that she monopolized the bell. And then she counted on her fingers how soon Mamma was expected.

So come home soon, little Mamma,

to
Lillan and Papa

4 November, 1905.

Dearest,

Richard B., to whom I gave my collected dramas a year ago, had not yet read *Kristina*. When he read it, he was amazed! "There is a rôle for Harriet! Why hasn't it been given on the stage?"

---

* It is a custom in the Swedish theatre to set aside one matinée or evening performance each season, or at the conclusion of a series of guest performances, entirely for the benefit of the star actor or actress.

And then he read *Gustav III!* More amazement! Now I have asked him to read *Damascus III.* I have to be discovered by those closest to me . . . But when will the others discover me?

Are you really coming next Monday? I can hardly believe it!

I assume Inez will come and meet you, and that I will have to wait until Tuesday. But don't hug your child to death when you wake her at ten in the evening on Monday. She just can't stay awake at that hour; and violent emotion and excitement are dangerous for children as well as for grown-ups.

Your
August Sg.

Following my guest appearances in Gothenburg I made a study and reconnaissance trip to Germany. As I mentioned earlier, Strindberg repeatedly brought up the idea of making the German stage my goal. But I myself was not particularly enthusiastic. It was the language that frightened me. To memorize a rôle in German might not be too difficult —but to get the feeling of and to think in a foreign tongue, I was afraid would be a well-nigh insurmountable obstacle. It would make my acting seem forced, unnatural and stilted. I had, of course, conquered the Swedish language completely; but then there was this difference: all my life I had been shuttling back and forth between Norway and Sweden—I was practically brought up in the two languages simultaneously.

However, many were working for my transplantation in Germany. Emil Schering, Strindberg's German translator, put me in touch with Vallentin, who at that time was the artistic director of the Deutsches Volkstheater in Vienna. Herr Vallentin was determined that I read *Simoon* before him in German. I learned the rôle in that language, but the words sounded ridiculous to me. When the reading was over, he remained silent for a considerable time. And then he offered me a five-year contract to appear in Berlin at his own theatre there, the Hebbeltheater, now renamed the Theater an der Königgrätzerstrasse.

He had intended that I make my first appearance there in his opening program, playing Marianne in Hebbel's *Herod and Marianne*. I ought, of course, to have been beside myself with joy at being offered such an opportunity, but I felt only anxiety and lacked any compelling desire. This does not mean that I did not realize the importance of his offer and the many advantages I would derive through this broader field of activity. But the deciding factor was that I had signed a five-year contract with Albert Ranft in Stockholm shortly before leaving for Germany. However, I did not think that he would refuse to release me, as he already had a long roster of artists under contract. Nevertheless he did! Moreover, his refusal was extremely emphatic—and there was nothing I could do to alter my fate. But perhaps this was all for the best, for a few months later Vallentin, who was to have introduced me on the German stage, died during a visit in Russia.

[Letters to Berlin and Vienna]

Saturday, 25 November, 1905.

Dear Harriet,

I can't . . . write about your child, for I have not seen her since you left. I presume this is in revenge for my being unable to receive her . . . but to take revenge on one who is innocent is wicked and brings its own punishment. . . .

I could not receive her because I have been obliged to sell some of the furniture for food and fuel. The piano is already gone.

You know that it was for the child's sake that I saddled myself with the apartment last fall. My intentions were the best, but I lacked the means to fulfill them. —And now this child shall be stolen from me like the others . . . But such is my fate, and I have had time to prepare myself . . . And now that the disaster has struck (last summer I went through the worst of it), I have a little more peace—with the greatest pain behind me . . . And I believe that we are now entering a new phase [of our lives]. We realized this the last time we met. To be friends, not lovers, is best—for I did not consider it right to be your lover without feeling my responsibilities. Another child would mean our ruin.

With love comes hate, you know that; but unselfish affection endures longer and is more precious. Since we have each returned to our freedom, why should we bind ourselves anew? Neither of us can tolerate bondage! Thus, since we hate any bond, why inflict our hate upon each other, as all married people and lovers do!

Let me be your friend, with obligations only to our child!

The rest is good will, asking no recompense, simply the pleasure of giving—which carries with it its own reward.

A bit of advice: Remain in Berlin, if you can.

The portrait is finished! Will be unveiled this evening.

That done, I can return to myself and my work.

Your friend

August Sg.

[Postcard]
Wednesday, 29 November, 1905.

Mamma dear. Today I am with Papa for dinner; and if you do not come home soon, I shall move back to Karlavägen.

Anne-Marie

[Postcard]
30 November, 1905.
[The date of the postmark]

Dear Mamma, I am again at Karlavägen and am eating dinner here, Thursday—(24 small pancakes!).

The sun is shining today and I have been out with aunt Inez! Elin is in good health and lives with her papa. Hope you are well.

Anne-Marie

30 November, 1905.

Dear Harriet,

In a few days I may be living at Stocksund, as Karlavägen 40 is in a state of dissolution. That is why I could not have the child with me.

Now as to your letter with your kind words in response to my harsh ones! Thank you!

I am, of course, following you with my thoughts and am inclined to advise you to enter Reinhardt's school, if only for appearances, let your self be "discovered"—and from there go on. The whole thing could be done in a couple of weeks!

But the main thing: Do you speak in German with the Scherings? And how does it sound? Have you conquered your antipathy to the language?

Ranft recently mentioned at a banquet for Nansen (Henning Berger and Fredrikson heard it!) that the King had offered him the New Theatre but that he had refused the offer because he would have to take orders from Bonde!

Tomorrow Mme. Nansen is again beginning her guest appearances at the Swedish Theatre! There you see Ranft's aversion to guest stars!

Lillan was here for dinner yesterday. I offered to have her stay here, but Inez thought this unnecessary as you would soon be back again.

Even if this trip should be a mere reconnaissance trip, use it to your best advantage and keep speaking German with Schering!

And thank you for your friendly letter! The weather here has been black as coal, but today the sun is shining. . . .

My portrait was inspected last Saturday by the Beethoven cronies and evoked general admiration and no unfavorable criticism. I am now posing for Eldh!

May all go well with you, dear friend, and welcome back to
Us!

30 November, 1905.

Dearest,
Since you find the bond between us still holds and no longer feel it oppressive—what do you say to this proposal, which after all is your own?
That I sell all the furniture and come down [to you] with Lillan and 3000 marks. Then we can settle down in Grunewald in a furnished apartment. I can take care of the child while you go on acting. Perhaps this will have to depend on what Vallentin has to say about your German speech?
But you must not consider yourself tied to me, and we will make a mutual pledge that the bond be terminated whenever you wish—although notice of termination should be given!
Think on this and sleep on it!
As to Reinhardt's school—you might join only the language class!

Your

August Sg.

It is terribly stale and insipid here!

2 December, 1905.

Harriet,
It seems as if our saga were at an end, and our mutual fates sealed . . . The destroying angel is stalking Karlavägen 40: the piano is gone; the Inferno painting also; and on Monday the rest of the paintings will have vanished. Lillan is abandoning me, too—she is obdurate and strange. . . .
The hardest thing of all is that my memories are fading, turning to ashes. . . .
Swanwhite is dead—long ago—*The Crown Bride* has lost her crown—The Daughter of Indra is beginning to thrive on the refuse heap and revels in the sufferings of mankind—The Easter Girl prefers the music hall to tragedy. Life is that way!
I no longer have any faith in our living together, for I do not believe in what has been. Perhaps you were the only one who divined me—at odd moments; yet. . . .
Where I am destined to go now, I do not know . . . It

will be away from here—but not downward . . . And I don't think I will ever again stand in your way—do not *want* to stand in your way!

Consider my last note unwritten, and resolve to seek your fortune elsewhere!

I am fed up with this world, and from now on I wish to devote myself to contemplating the end and what follows the end. . . .

Life has been nothing but lies and fraud and vanity and leaves me with no feeling of loss, only loathing.

Should I live much longer, I assume that our relationship will go up in smoke like the rest, and that the child shall be as much a stranger to me as the others.*

It will be a relative happiness to reach the other side.

August Sg.

4 December, 1905.

Dear child,

The moods keep changing, and our letters do not express our true feelings. But it does not matter!

Berlin presents obstacles! There were obstacles at first everywhere: in Helsingfors and Gothenburg—yet both ended with glory, and even a little gold.

You don't know how Berlin would seem to you if you had a home of your own, with children, servants, friends, an engagement and an income!

If the Germans are uncouth, they nevertheless appreciate refinement. Look at Duse!

Teach them refinement and they will be grateful!

If, however, you have no more illusions about your art—then it either means that you, as a woman, are so wholesome that you place children and home above everything else, or that you will progress to artistry that is truly independent—which is poetry itself!

If you feel no compulsion to write, then choose the former,

---

* Strindberg felt deeply the separation from his other children.

but marry—marry someone with money! You were not born for adventure!

There you have my opinion!

All you need now is a foothold and a little encouragement, then your head will be above water again. Strange that you do not converse with the Scherings in German—and that you should choose the trifling *Simoon*.

Things are happening that are not mentioned in your letters, but which I can imagine. . . .

Collect yourself, get your bearings, and you will advance with greater assurance.

Do not let yourself be influenced by the first one who comes along.

Cease going to the theatre, get some rest, distract yourself, and bide your time! But work for a definite goal! Otherwise you will disintegrate!

Can't you appear in *The Wild Duck* in Swedish immediately? Forget about *Simoon*—you will get no sympathy!

Your
August Sg.

6 December, 1905.

Dear child,

Listen to this advice! In order to learn whether Ranft has merely been talking, telegraph at once from Vienna and demand a definite answer. If he makes trouble, you have Germany to fall back upon. You see how they receive you, how they carry you upon their shoulders, and beg you to remain— even register you in the census books.

That you have to endure Strindberg on your Vienna trip is something that will necessarily come to an end; but use him, he is glad to be of service and to help his Queen of Hearts. Later, however, go on to Maeterlinck, Sophocles, Puck, Ibsen —whatever you desire, even Hauptmann, but not *Simoon!*

I asked Lillan to come and live with me; but without servants it would be impossible. . . .

August Sg.

8 *December, 1905.*
At midnight.

Dear Harriet,

Do you think we could ever be separated from each other, the way our lives are grafted together? When you feel anxiety far away in a strange land, my heart beats in my breast up here [in the North] as if it were yours.

Sometimes I feel your warm breath caressing my cheek; and then I have a feeling that you speak my name in a friendly spirit.

Now and then I have you inside my coat, and then sense it as if I were actually you. . . .

Would not the operation of tearing each other out of our lives be a painful one?

What kind of Christmas awaits us—a fortnight from now?

August Sg.

Arrived home from Germany, I had much work ahead of me. I was to make guest appearances again in Helsingfors.

Before I left for Helsingfors in the spring of 1906, Strindberg had told me that the royalties for those plays of his that might be given during my engagement there, were to be assigned to the children of his first marriage, who were all living in Finland. No doubt he suffered many a time from being unable to assist them in a more generous manner. As soon as his financial position became a little more secure, he promptly made up for past delinquencies.

Almost throughout his life, Strindberg had had to struggle with economic hardships. Only just before he died, did a gleam of light brighten his existence. Once during our marriage he thought himself a Croesus when Bonnier paid him a lump sum of 6,000 crowns for one of his manuscripts. He seemed to think that this money would last forever! Whenever I was in need of money he was always quick to give it to me. On several occasions, when he was short of money, he sold some of his paintings through the aid of a friend.

He rarely spoke of his previous marriages. Whenever he mentioned Siri von Essen, he did so in a kindly, well-intentioned and correct manner.

Strindberg made me vow never to read *The Confessions of a Fool* or to play *Miss Julie*. This promise I have kept.

[Letter to Helsingfors]

13 *March*, 1906.

Dear child,

. . . . . .

Duncan is coming to the Olympia May 1–7. Let her, as far as I am concerned. Am not going and don't care to meet her. Berger and Engström got hold of Craig and drove around for about 24 hours . . . I didn't see them again.

. . . . . .

Now the dramas begin to grow in me again—grand and heavy—ripening; and I shall write them all. . . .

Easter is approaching—chastisement in the air—suffering—the cross. . . .

Your

August Sg.

17 *March* 1906.

Dear friend,

Today, the 17th, your letter dated the 5th arrived—eight days en route.

How strange that people must suffer pain in seeking the beautiful . . . But what are we to do? Flee! Where?

Things look bad for me, too. Here hate is rampant, and it stems from a fear that I might be given justice and come into my own. It is possible that I will not come out of this alive.

Despite it all, I am writing dramas . . . that is my calling.

Your

August Sg.

17 March 1906.
Dear child,
You are so restless that I don't know where I have you. . . .
Nothing new except that Craig was here. We did not understand each other, and so I sent Berger to speak English with him and help him. With what result I haven't heard. Berger told him that we had no interest in ballet. Sv. D. lashed out at Duncan. Craig gave the impression of being in love with her and, like Schering, had vowed that she would come here. I discouraged the project. And now they are gone—with a horrible impression of Sweden and the Swedes. . . . We [purposely] made ourselves as horrible as we could. Craig was like Oscar Wilde—der war mir zu schön.*
                                    Your
                                          August Sg.

18 March, 1906.
Dear Harriet,
Last night—Saturday-Sunday the 17th–18th—I was in Helsingfors, and I recall something about a Järnefelt—that's all I can remember.

    .   .   .   .

Well, the dramas are coming [to me] again now—the first one in verse . . . I can't write any more to you now; I feel as if strangers had broken the contact between us.
And Easter is approaching!
                                    Your
                                          August Sg.
Sibelius is welcome to do *Swanwhite*. *The Crown Bride* may be billed as a fairy play or anything else.

19 March, 1906.
Dear child,
I have developed a headache because of all your vicissitudes —I who am usually never bothered by anything like that. And

---

* He was too beautiful [handsome] for me.

my nights are restless, too. And added to this, the hatred! My ears ring all day long from the gossip.

Tor Hedberg attacked Eldh's bust in bronze, now being exhibited in Uppsala. But the committee bought it for The National Museum!!!

Eight votes out of nine—the ninth was Wirsén's.—That is why people are raging worse than ever; and if there is any chance of preventing it, it will be done! However, my aspirations do not lie in that direction—I have another ambition: to write dramas!

I am afraid of the governor-general's banquet.* It is politics, and the Finns have no love for the Russians. But you yourself have to be the judge in the matter! However, do not let yourself be duped so that you have to leave the country!

Lillan is well-behaved and has grown beautiful again. A quiet, melancholy feeling of missing her Mother is becoming to her. Now, for the first time, she has a consciousness of her loss.

New Swedish Adventures is now being printed!

And then the dramas will begin!

I am afraid I shall have to remain in the city this summer, but it doesn't matter as long as I can write!

Your friend
August Sg.

22 March, 1906.

Dear Harriet,

Lillan is here every day! Now she resembles Greta again—just as the last time you were in Finland! Isn't that strange!

Next Sunday we celebrate her birthday with a drive to Djurgården—exactly as before—and then dinner. . . .

Berger has gone abroad—and for good. He, too, is being divorced.

Eldh takes great pleasure in his image of me. Rubenson stated that the New Theatre has asked for a replica.

Next week there will be a vote in the riksdag on my pension, and it is expected to go through.

See: Notes.

Next Tuesday, the 27th, Aulin's Quartet has invited itself here to celebrate the anniversary of Beethoven's death. Stenhammar may accompany them.

Axel and Richard B. were here the day before yesterday; we cultivated the 7th Symphony with "The Waves of Music," also the Ninth, which will be given next week. It is gratifying to see that Beethoven endures—everything else is so transient.

Isadora has had Craig write to Henning Berger that she would build a box seat on the stage for me—as I *must* see her. I answered B. that I did not want to see her. If you are not here to save me, I am leaving town.

Schering writes that Craig is Isadora's lover and is ruining her, and therefore he is little respected. Craig brought with him here "England's foremost composer" Shaw.

Engström admired Craig's paintings.

Give my greetings to Greta and say: I hope that they will receive a little money from Wetzer for the spring, from my plays.

No other letter of authority is necessary.

All good things to you now.

Your friend
August Sg.

29 March, 1906.

Dear friend,

You always have it difficult. If it is only in the beginning, it doesn't matter so much. But give no thought to my plays, nor to making big money.

The day before yesterday, we celebrated the anniversary of Beethoven's death. Aulin's Quartet—Stenhammar did not come. Axel had to play the accompaniments to the Kreutzer Sonata and the C minor trio—these two are Beethoven's most beautiful works. Our spirits were high and devout. Bergh, Nordström and Axel—none else!

To honor Aulin I had given him your chair at the supper table. But as soon as I turn my back—the chair is replaced! Ebba had done it! There you have a friend!

Lillan has been ailing! Inez difficult, and seems unfriendly.

But say nothing, for then she will take revenge! I just can't talk to her; everything is at cross purposes!

Soon the summer will be here, and then I shall leave and go swimming in the Baltic—and write dramas. . . . Thus we shan't really be seeing each other until autumn! . . . .

So farewell for a while!

Your friend
August Sg.

1 *April, 1906.*

Dear You,

Today I finished the prologue in verse for my new drama.*
. . . Strange: In the surging joy during the conception of it, I picture the drama throughout as ethereal, grand and beautiful! [But] when I write it down, it loses all this and becomes something else. It is almost a transgression to write. To put things into words is to degrade—to turn poetry into prose! To reduce to the commonplace, in brief . . . That is why I suffer from writing and gladly turn my back on what I have written. . . .

The thoughts of summer are beginning to stir in me. . . . To Furusund, or at least the Baltic.

Svennberg visited me yesterday! The distaff side is weak for next season at the Swedish Theatre. He has an engagement there; and the male side is strong. Ranft is on edge and is soon leaving for abroad.

Well, that is about all! Soon Easter is here!

Your friend
August Sg.

4 *April, 1906.*

Dear child,

Of course I am not afraid of Duncan! I am merely "afraid" of persistent people!

Yesterday, the third, I went to Liding Isle Bridge with Gyllensköld. The cove was blue, the sun was shining.—Chambertin—oysters—alles! Drove home beneath the stars. . . .

* The prologue to *A Dream Play* was written in 1906.

I am now writing the drama with spring in my blood. Most of it in verse. . . .
Am wearing my spring overcoat—the window is open all day—I can breathe again!
Drachman is expected here! Burgundy!
How goes it with you? You are so silent! Are you receiving my letters?

Your friend
August Sg.

Note: Ranft is soon leaving for abroad!

7 April, 1906.

Dear You,

I read today your postcard to Lillan, in which you hint at an early return. That is why I am writing this—in case you are still there.

I have reverted to being alone again, and aloneness is the better way. Having people around you is nothing but an illusion that one constantly refutes and then renews.

The riksdag came to no decision about my pension, but it will be taken up again in May.

I am reading Shakespeare for want of anything else. *Cymbeline* and *A Winter's Tale*. I think they are terrible—yet there is something about them that I can't explain: a red thread that keeps the tatters together. I discovered nothing new in them.

Well—and this is all!

Your friend
August Sg.

Palm Sunday 8 April, 1906.

Dear You,

This morning I woke up with a definite urgency to break loose from Karlavägen and go out to Stocksund. Since I already know that I shall be alone this summer, it is less painful to prepare for it than to sit and wait for something I know beforehand will not come to pass.

Now we shall see how my fate develops.

An occultist happened to glimpse at my hand and discovered two life lines—indicating a long life span. But the mount of Venus was not too clear, and so Tannhäuser still has to go through a few things. . . .

The usual horrors of summer lie ahead. Companions are an illusion, no doubt, but solitude is still worse. The middle road would unquestionably be the best.

Lillan is pale; she is pining away out of grief for you—she may be suffering from all our discord. She complains of being tired; she may already be tired of it all! She often explains that she likes Papa and Mamma.

Was will jetzt werden?*

Your
August Sg.

15 April, 1906.

Dear child,

Easter went well! What a miracle! Now I have nothing to reproach myself for.

However, now it is Easter [for me] the whole year, year in and year out.

I want to move, but I can't; feel as if I were walking in space, I turn dizzy, lose track of thoughts and memories, stored in this apartment; I am being put under the yoke of strangers—their tastes and whims—have to flatter their frailties, their mongrels and their servants. I feel it has come to this: Either stay, or earnestly seek out unknown regions—away from all this—over to the other side!

My drama escaped me . . . disappeared . . . lost in emptiness! But [I] must take hold of something else. The novel intrigues me most. I detest the theatre. Pose—superficiality—contrivance! Read *The [Taming of the] Shrew* by Shakespeare. Gruesome. Circus . . . false, clumsy, lacking in truth. Think of a public that allows itself to have its vision so distorted. And how can Borgström possibly make anything out of this

---

* What will happen next?

hollow, empty rôle? Most people go around like stupid cattle that you can beguile into believing anything. Those who have the misfortune to have had their eyes opened—they ought to take leave of this world.

Balzac's type of novel intrigues me most just now. On the style of *Alone*. It permits one to explain oneself, expand, interpret individuals, take a thorough look at their insides.

The Easter egg from you came this evening, and Lillan was present. With the table heaped with eggs, we both laughed aloud, and Papa couldn't tell, even with his glasses, whether the last one—no bigger than a pea—really was the last egg.

Tomorrow we are having dinner here—with asparagus and meringue glacée—with Inez and Alf present as well.

19 degrees in the shade! I should not be surprised if Vesuvius * had something to do with this!

And that's that!

Come quickly now and give me courage to move out to Stocksund, for I must get away from here!

Your friend
August Sg.

18 *April*, 1906.

Dear You,

Albert Ranft was here with me Easter Monday, from seven in the evening until two in the morning. He spoke about you with the greatest expectations and contracted for several of my plays, among them *Swanwhite*, *The Crown Bride* and *The Dance of Death*.

Many things were discussed, but I can't speak about this in a letter.

Enclosed you see Täckholmen and the Cabin where I made gold in 1900, but quickly abandoned in order to meet you on July 1 (?) on Banérgatan. People don't like to see that we cling together. You will see that they will not rest until they have "saved" you. Since their first attempt was a failure, they are raging—from pure love of humanity—and they consider it their sacred duty to murder me. That is how unselfish they are!

* It erupted in April, 1906.

As I do not hold life dear, I am prepared for any eventuality, especially since most of my work is finished.

Lillan seems to divine what is coming and consoles me with her kindness . . . which, however, always touches me as if it were a farewell, the farewell that must come. . . . Self-deception seems a necessary evil in order to exist; for when one's eyes occasionally are opened and see humanity in all its horrible nakedness, one shudders—and wants to get away from it all, even though one asks nothing whatever from anybody. . . .

The theatre is still repugnant to me and I now want to be Balzac. But first I must move and experience new surroundings.

Young Ranft acted Benjamin in *Easter*, I see. I didn't know that. How was he?

And now: *The Crown Bride* on the 24th!

Your friend
August Sg.

26 April, 1906.

Dear child,

What is the matter with you, since you keep complaining so? I am in complete ignorance and can't offer you a word of consolation. You want to die! You, too! Can it be a sympathetic feeling [between us]? . . . Perhaps we could help each other to go on living?

Persons of our prominence are never surrounded by friends, only by secret police who worm out the significance of the smallest word. Loneliness is the lot of the famous. Hate is their reward, and treachery their bread. The thing that attracts others is not friendship but rather the opposite. Flies pick out mirrors and gilt surfaces to speck because they are glossy and shine brightly.

Perhaps you ask too much of life. It yields its return, but like the field—through sweat and hard labor, and with many disappointments.

That something has happened I can understand, but have no idea what. You have broken away from me, I can feel it.

Only recently I had a dream that told me that you had met Fru v. E. [Siri von Essen], or been near her.

However, thank you for *The Crown Bride*; and extend my gratitude to the director and all the artists, as well as the stage crew.

Soon you will be here again, you know, and then it will all be over!

Now that Ranft is to produce three of my plays this fall and next spring, I wonder whether I might continue to live here!

Lillan is counting the days!

August Sg.

28 *April*, 1906.

Dear You,

It was you who were responsible for *The Crown Bride*, and I thank you for it! Now only *Swanwhite* remains, and then the whole program is realized. . . .

Why are you sad? In Indian books of wisdom, there is a saying that an inexplicable sadness foreshadows a coming happiness.

But I confess that there is something else that affects me most painfully. When one gets a glimpse into the lives of others—and sees all the horrors that are hidden beneath a charming, respectable surface—then one wants to die! . . . .

I am struggling with my education but am making slow progress. In the end religion means this to me: The hope of a better world, a conviction that we will be set free, and putting our trust in God! Here we have little to expect—"for what I want to do, I don't do; only that which I hate, I do."— But now it is no longer I who do it—it is the sinfulness that dwells in me. . . .

—For my delight is in the law of the Lord in my inward parts, but I see another law in my flesh that struggles against the law that is in my spirit. . . .

Poor creature that I am, who shall deliver me from this body of death? That is the plaint that is chorused by all mankind!

I paid your child a visit this morning, brought some presents. "Papa must stay!" she said. It is so hard to go then! . . . Homeless—and so young! Perhaps that is what is meant to be! Now I can look forward to the summer, having received some money . . . And it will probably be Furusund because of the aquamarine water there.

Next Thursday you will be here again! I rejoice principally for Lillan's sake—for I myself am most of the time an outsider!

August Sg.

The summer of 1906 Anne-Marie and I again went to Hornbaek in Denmark. We remained there only a brief time, since my throat began to trouble me and I had to have a change of air. I decided to go to Åre in western Sweden, not far from the Norwegian border.

Strindberg was unable to break away from Karlavägen and he stayed in his apartment throughout the summer.

[Letter to Hornbaek]

2 June, 1906.

My dear little friends,

First of all thanks for your lovely letters. We have begun to have Rävsnäs summer here: 8°, gloom during the day, rain and mist. But the poor fellow who remains in the city does not complain, for he can breathe, can move about, and is not bothered by the dust, the flies and such things.

. . . . . .

I shall have my novel finished by Monday,* yet I have no longing for the country. Instead I have ordered floor covering (cork) for the hall and my study.

. . . . . .

* *The Scapegoat* [translated into English by Arvid Paulson].

As usual, alone, yet I suffer no want; but when the others [in the house] have moved [to the country], then one begins to feel it. The house is already empty, the Jansons and the Frölichs have left—and now I can't help missing the child that used to cry.

All good things to you, and think of me!

Your friend

August Sg.

5 June, 1906.

Dear You,

It would seem as though I might be bitter, sitting here all alone, with everybody in Denmark and in Sweden-Norway having the right to caress my child—everyone in this world but I can settle down in Hornbaek and enjoy your company—all but I!

Yet I am not embittered, for I am civilized; and I know how things would be if we lived together. You, too, know it, and that you would not be satisfied to spend your time with your family and in the theatre exclusively and I refuse to accept any sacrifices, and to create martyrs. The pain you feel in my presence you blame me for despite the fact that it has its roots in the impossibility of two persons to round out each other's lives.

Therefore, better to let well enough alone, since there is no chance for improvement.

Whitsuntide—alone—rain—cold, etc. The new cork covering in my room is smooth as a meadow and gives me great pleasure. The hall, too, and the corridor in its fresh cleanliness—with five years of dust removed.

Tomorrow I shall have finished my novel!

And after that. . . .

Everything has ceased to be, nothing happens, deathly silence throughout the house, life is no longer functioning . . . that is the time one needs religion in order not to die. . . .

Your friend

August Sg.

11 June, 1906.

You dear two,
Nothing to do, alone! The novel has been sold to *Idun*—1500 crowns. Why don't we join hands and enjoy boredom together on my great wealth? I would like to live at Drottningholm in order to relive my childhood, to walk about in civilized surroundings without any contact with living creatures, to get the feel of my native land, to discover its origins in history, legend and song, and to be able to write the dedication prologue for the National Theatre. Or perhaps rather Gripsholm?

Lindberg was here last Saturday night(!). He told me that "the King wept and took up the applause for the prologue." Lindberg had just come from Ibsen's funeral, but despite this was sympathetic. The man has something elevating about him; he is not unsophisticated—but then he has lived a thousand lives in the creations of great poets.

The Scherings are at Mölle—opposite you. He is displeased, and so he will probably soon be moving across [to the Danish coast].

The calendar gives this proverb for today:
  Begrabe deine Toten tief in dein Herz hinein
  So werden sie dem Leben lebend'ge Tote sein.

Watch out for Lillan. I keep reading horrible [newspaper] accounts from Denmark!

                                    Your
                                    August Sg.

22 June, 1906.

My dearest ones,
Where are you? I feel as if you were drifting further and further away and your images fade: I scarcely remember what you look like—your voices.

Summer begins today, and the sun turns its face upon the darkness. Evenings, a ray of light—one single beam—falls into the dining-room, lingers on the sideboard.

If you are not happy where you are, then come back here.

I'll rent a place for the summer for you, and will come to see you on Saturdays.

After an insufferable heat today, a cooling rain falls . . . the only joy left us in the city.

Your
August Sg.

After a brief visit with Strindberg while passing through Stockholm, I was on my way to Åre in Western Sweden.

[Letters to Åre]

6 July, 1906.

My dears,

I hardly had time to greet you before you were gone. And then I developed pains in my throat and chest, accompanied by fever, last night; and today everything has been black for me. Today is really the first sultry day, and the apartment seems unfriendly, gloomy. I usually ask myself: What have I done?—Don't know.—Shall I go away?—Where? . . . Everything is the same everywhere.

I have discovered that I have made gold for the last ten years but thrown it away because it always came out black as soot, brown like snuff. But I haven't the strength to make any fuss—no one would believe it anyhow. I am sending you the formula to use after my death.

FORMULA

Iron vitriol
Copper nitrate } Extremely weak solutions.
Silver nitrate

(Heat, preferably with a piece of paper in the bottom of the cooking utensil).

May be varied extensively by one solution or one precipitate as reagent.

That is the secret; in this way any metal can be produced by means of its own solution or precipitate reagent.

But gold is produced by one copper and one silver salt, precipitated with iron vitriol, or with oxalic acid, or with tartaric acid ammoniac, or with stannous chloride, or with quicksilver oxidul nitrate. Save this letter for the fun of it.

The goldplated silver you saw is made in this manner: The silver leaves are immersed in a weak solution of $Cu\ So_4$ plus $Fe\ So_4$ plus $Na\ So_2$ and heated. Then they are dipped in borax and dissolved in water: a *blue* liquid and a *brown*, gleaming substance—which is the character of a gold solution—are the result.

All good to you, and think of me!

Your
August Sg.

Postcard dated 6 August, 1906.
[The date of the postmark]

Dear You, Mamma read wrong. I wrote that I have a camera, but can't use it because my hands are bleeding. But I shall have an enlargement *made* of this picture of grandmother. I must ask you to answer the two questions I put to you, and also this one: Shall I send the registered letter to Åre, or not?— Autumn has come—15°. The season is starting . . . Welcome back!

Your
August Sg.

7 August, 1906.

Dear child,

Money exists only when in hand; therefore I may as well send it now as later.

With friendship
August Sg.

[Postcard to Anne-Marie Strindberg, Totten via Åre]

11 August, 1906.
[The date of the postmark.]

Little child of Jämtland! Yes—this is how it is: Your grandfather's grandfather was a curate in Revsund [in that province]

—the railroad station just before Åre. His son went to Stockholm and engaged in the grocery business. But he also wrote plays for the theatre: three are printed and can be found in the library. Members of the Strindberg family still live in Jämtland —people in modest circumstances. Actually the name is derived from Strinna or Strinda near Multrå in Ångermanland.*

Your

August Sg.

During the latter part of 1906 I received no letter from Strindberg until the second week of December.

10 December, 1906.

Harriet,

. . . .

You know why I left—to give you your freedom. I have a feeling that you have not used it. Am I mistaken?

August Sg.

From December, 1906, until the spring of 1907 Strindberg did not write many letters to me. Little by little, after untold dissensions, the bond had been broken; yet the following letter is proof that he still had thoughts of me:

12 May, 1907.

Need I write to you? You know very well both what I think and what I feel. What you wrote to me, I already knew— and who tortured you, although no one had told me. Whenever you suffer I am by your side and suffer with you. But when you are glad, I cannot always share your joy since life has placed you on the side of the enemy. I cannot rejoice over an unjust conquest gained at my expense!

I am now trying to get used to my deep loneliness during

---

* Strindberg had asked Harriet Bosse to investigate whether there was a locality in Jämtland beginning with *Strind*, explaining that Strind (in the Eddas) has the meaning of *earth*.

the summer and expect nothing more from life. Everything has proved ephemeral, perishable and transient. Even my child is gone from me—strangers have turned her away from me . . . But it is a grace not to feel the pain of my loss, with the sundering of every bond I am freeing myself from my captivity.

Let me keep my silence! In silence I find it easier to be near you in spirit—as you appear to me, without any alien quality woven into your being. . . .

I can't make contact with your home because unsympathetic persons are welcomed there—and yet your home is such a perfection of beauty that one might think it was I who had furnished it with my good wishes for you and the child! I can't speak with you for I have nothing to say that can be said; I have no yearning to see you, for I see you whenever I wish— the way I wish to see you. . . .

People and life tried to separate us, in a worldly way, but I think that we will meet in spite of it—some time, somewhere . . . for there is doubtless a relationship between us, and we shall therefore always be akin. . . .

Your
Nameless

The following two letters were addressed to Åre, where I also spent the summer of 1907:

[To Anne-Marie Strindberg]

11 July, 1907.

Dear little child,

No, I have not been away from Stockholm, but my longing has somehow drifted to the verdant island of my youth. . . .

And I have followed you in my thoughts, sometimes with uneasiness, as though you were sick, or in danger, and I am still not free of that anxiety. . . .

Would have sent you some money for the summer, but your needy sisters and brother had to have money for their stay in the country, as did Karin for her trip to Greta's. Greta, whom I gave 1000 crowns as a dowry, is now married and lives on Blid Isle.

We have seen no sign of summer here, the first streetlight has already been lit, and the first star (Capella, the little goat) has been glimpsed through the dining-room window.

We have been working hard to establish a theatre in Stockholm where my best plays—which no one here wants to produce—can be staged. . . .

Sibelius is now writing music for *Swanwhite* and is enraptured, Wetzer writes.

My friend Schering is left alone in Grunewald, grieving for wife and child who have gone to America. But he is carrying on the work for me and has had *Wetterleuchten* [stormclouds] accepted. Reinhardt himself is acting the leading rôle.

Now you know all the news; and as I presume that you will read this letter aloud to Mamma, she too will know how I am faring. . . .

All good to you both! If you should need anything in the way of clothes—just write!

Your friend
August Sg.

25 July, 1907.

My dear ones,

To meet only to part is more pain than joy, but since we both must live in the same city, we may as well pull together as turn into ghosts of memories that one might be afraid to greet when seeing them . . . That is why I ask you if you two would like to come to Sunday dinner at three o'clock; and I pray that you answer by telegram, for there will not be time to do it by letter!

I really need you as I am about to write something fine for the New Theatre or some other theatre!

Your
August Sg.

[After I had returned to Stockholm, Strindberg wrote the following letters to me.]

TO HARRIET BOSSE 165

19 October, 1907.

Harriet,

. . . . . .

If anything should happen to Lillan we shall forever reproach ourselves for every single moment she has suffered pain and annoyance, even if we were not to blame.

I long for her all the time—you know that—but I can't help thinking that for those moments of longing she is the one who really suffers, from loneliness—and that she is aching for someone to love her. . . .

This is what makes it impossible for me to have a moment of happiness.

August Sg.

With this, money for hat and coat, etc.

Date unknown. [1907.]

Let us not meet—it is too painful.
This eternal leave taking, now in its seventh year. . . . haven't I suffered enough?
I have broken with the world you live in, forever.
My child was stolen from me while in her mother's womb, and since then her soul has been stolen. . . .
Let there be an end to this. Keep company with your friends, who are my enemies, but touch no longer my fate. I shall not take revenge, but as long as I do the just thing, I shall be protected.
Enjoy your freedom for which you have ached so long—I do not care to bind you or to be the jailer whom one may feel free to murder!

Farewell!

Strindberg's *Swanwhite* had been accepted for production by the Swedish Theatre in Stockholm. We rehearsed the play, but it was abandoned and was not produced there until many years later. I did not appear in the play then.

I conclude with the following letters from Strindberg, and prefer not to augment them with any commentary. As the letters themselves indicate, some of them were written as a consequence of my second marriage. What I suffered during this period—knowing that Strindberg constantly was thinking of me, day and night—is impossible for me to describe. I wanted to sever completely the bond between us and earnestly pleaded with him not to write to me—but it did not help. He sent me a book, *The Tale of Knight Huon*. The fly leaf bore the following inscription:

Give me more beauty to write about, Swanwhite,
give me a new pen of gold, Chrysaëtos.

[*April, 1908*].
You do not answer my direct question about *Swanwhite*. Have you drifted away from her? If you are tired of her, just tell me! I am not anxious to have it produced by Ranft, and it is only for your sake I offered the play to him. Herodias's daughter is much more in your genre, isn't it? I shall accept your silence, if it continues, as a sign of indifference, and shall demand the return of the play.

Sometimes I think that you laugh at my childish play . . . You may do so, but it is a sin! You are angry with me because you saw a [certain] play at the Intimate Theatre. I had warned you against [seeing] it.—It was a painful piece of imagery with which I wanted to write you and Lillan out of my heart! I wanted to suffer in advance some of the anguish that was waiting for me.

But in it there was neither a relative nor even a maidservant. On the other hand, there was an altar to Home and Memory for you both. The beauty of *that* you failed to see!

I think that now is the time to disentangle myself from your net! There is only one way out, and that cannot possibly fail! You have just tried the method, without success. I shall succeed.

(Written in pencil outside the envelope)

Castegren has written to Ranft in Berlin regarding *Swanwhite* and Sibelius's music at Schlesinger Editeur.

[April, 1908.]
Say one word! I have heard nothing! But I read a good deal in the glances of people I met on the streets and elsewhere this morning!

If it be so, then know that I feel both my responsibility and my obligations—which are enduring as long as you are faithful to me in your thoughts, words, desires and glances, in everything. . . .

Castegren has not replied! There must be some meaning to that!

Say one word! You must think that I know what the whole world knows, but you are wrong! In one way I do know, intuitively, but not as everybody else knows! I have heard nothing!!!

[8 April, 1908.]
When you told me last Saturday that you were engaged I almost knew it beforehand. But I could not wish you happiness as that is something I cannot believe in, for it does not exist. I felt no anxiety for the child, for I believe in God.

I would, however, have liked to bid you goodbye. And now I wish to thank you—despite all—for everything, for the months of spring seven years ago . . . when I, after twenty years of misery, was allowed to see a little of the bright side of life. But I could not bring myself to write . . . I received apprehensions that made me hesitant. Sunday went by, and so did Monday, in work and quiet resignation. You noticed that I, exactly a year ago, ceased making visits, and know the reasons for that.

And yesterday Tuesday came! When I went out in the morning, I thought it was Sunday. The city had changed in appearance, and so had the rooms here in the apartment. You had died! And then began a glorification of memories for the rest of the day, twelve hours, in the space of which I lived through these past seven years.

Reproaches, pangs of conscience for all that I had failed to do, every harsh word—all, all, exactly as when someone dear to you had passed out of life. The less beautiful was obliterated, only what was lovely remained.

In view of the fact that all was over [between us], I had the definite impression: Dead! I mourned you as one who was dead, and I could not feel a desire to have you back, since you no longer existed. . . .

In my memory I saw the Easter Girl, *To Damascus*, Djurgården with the military salute and the King's greeting, [Hotel] Rydberg and Drottningholm.

I wept—not from the pain of losing you this time, but from the happiness that these moments of you, and with you, had given me. . . .

Today is the day of *Swanwhite!* It will be given tonight with Sibelius's music. I have received it from you—as I have said in writing—and although I sometimes have doubted it, I do believe it! That is how I see you now, Harriet, after your death, despite the fact that I always knew who you were, your nature, your inclinations. I have explained this in *Kristina*. Your *Swanwhite*, which I received from you—and you from me—and which you never came to act. . . .

Today I have divined as if . . . you were not dead! . . . .

My thoughts and goodwill follow you, and I am—despite everything—forever your friend and your child's.

But I feel anxiety for you—and something is happening that I cannot grasp . . . In fact, I have not understood any part of this last incident; but as I am forbidden to write to you, perhaps there is not even any necessity for it!

If you only knew how dangerous it is to tangle with human fates and to play with thunder and lightning!

To free oneself from the tangle is such a painful undertaking . . . you know how tedious and agonizing the process was for us! You are satisfied if you can evoke a man's interest —and then drop him. But there is more to it than turning on your heel and walking away . . . There is much more!

Just one thing! Let me have Lillan when you marry! Or do you want me to go far away?

To be passing each other here on the streets is painful and unclean. And the child should be kept away from all this!

Do you want me to go away? I believe I am a disturbing influence, and from this apartment emanate invisible threads that carry inaudible soundwaves which, nevertheless, reach their destination. . . .

Our bond is not yet broken, but it has to be severed . . . otherwise we shall be contaminated . . . You remember our first days [together] when the evil radiation from souls, alien to ours, played havoc with us merely through thinking of us. . . .

Tell me what you wish, but arrange it so that we are not pulled down into an abyss of darkness—of which I am fearful . . . A telegram pertaining to your *Swanwhite* just arrived—despite all!

Why did you not wish to be what I created you to be in my imagery? I could not have pulled you down, as you said! That I don't believe!

One word more, just one! Do not sink down, Harriet! For then I shall weep again over the transience of all that is beautiful. . . .

Your *Swanwhite*, which I received from you, and you from me!

9 April, 1908.

I must finish my letter and tell you plainly, in a few words, what I mean. You know I have been wanting to regain my freedom and to give yours back to you; and each time you turned away from me and gave your affections to someone else, I was free until the moment you again began to think of me. Then it grew cloudy, and I reproached myself afterwards. . . .

That is why I beg you now, when there is no chance of return: Do not think of me, neither with good will nor evil, do not speak of me ever, do not mention my name—and if others should do it, refuse [to listen] or keep silent!

I do not wish to live this double life, entrapped in others' eroticism . . . I would rather mourn you as dead than remember you as the wife of another man. And you bring disharmony into your own life, for it is only we two who "live on an astral plane." Lightning can strike behind and in all directions, and one of us could die—perhaps [even] the one you would miss most. . . .

You know very well how often you have been ill and even felt tired of living (suicide mania). The cause? Why, all those whose feelings you have aroused, have cast back on you the currents you have evoked, and you in turn have suffered. That you were not killed one time (1901) was a miracle; and that I did not kill myself a still greater one.

Sometimes I think that you intended to do away with me. Dear child, there was nothing I could have wished for more . . . but what would have been gained? I, like other sinners, would, I suppose, have been washed clean as a corpse . . . my soul would live on in those of my works that will survive, my name on the billboards in the city would always remind you of me, our child would perhaps for a time torture you by the mention of my name—yet not for too long! Thus, there is no help except for me who was born with a repulsion for life and gladly would depart from it—although in a decent manner. . . .

Sometimes I think it would be altogether more right and better to part in hatred, in real hate; then that would be the end. You may answer: We have parted in hate . . . time and time again! And then we met again! Why do you keep playing with love, you who have suffered so much because of it and spread so much misery and sorrow (I know one man who died as a result!)? I once believed you had been playing with me, too, but it seemed unreasonable that a lovely young girl would give herself to an old man merely for an opportunity to murder him. And that we found it so hard to part indicated nevertheless a certain liking.

I beg you now: Leave me in peace! In my sleep I am defenseless, like the rest, irresponsible . . . and I am ashamed of myself afterwards—now I think of it as a crime. . . .

10 April, 1908.
This morning I have recovered our correspondence—which actually never was lost! When I said so, it was a *lapsus linguae*

(mere talk, in anger), for I *never* lied to you, but I kept silent occasionally, justifiably.

When one enters into a new union it is customary to return [all] letters, or to burn them. I have glanced through ours and have had a couple of sublime hours. I find in these letters the very finest in us, our souls in holiday dress, as life in the flesh seldom is. It is no poetic imagery; it is true to life. There is no posing [in them], no illusions—and if by illusion is meant something unreal, then this is the very highest reality.

That is how it was—not merely gave the appearance of being so! Shall I burn all this? I am sending you a sampling of some of mine. I have a couple of hundred of yours, all beautiful, as are mine; not an unbeautiful word, not an ugly thought! You see, my child, in your letters you live and reveal yourself as "the great woman" I suspected you to be. That the every-day type does not fulfill these characteristics is the fault of life itself, which is so grim and which provides such unlovely situations.

Words and the tongue are so impure that they are unable to express the most sublime. The written word on white paper is purer! To burn your letters would be to burn you—and that I cannot do! Tell me what you desire!

But forget me! Give me back my freedom, which I need; you shall need yours, too, in your new alliance! Do this, or we shall all be haunted by unhappiness—all of us! I cannot live in crime and disharmony—in sin! . . . .

When I read the poor photographer's letter to me—after you, by a mere word, had saved him and his family*—that he ended his letter with a blessing, I wept for "the little heart" and I felt as if he were a better human being than I—and as if I were the most despicable being of all! But am I? Am I?

[*April, 1908.*]
It is now seven years since we were married! Could this be the seven fires . . . could it be that the white dove is coming with the seven roses from the ear [of grain]? Why do we "meet" only now—when it is too late?

* See letter dated 29 March, 1901, to which incident it no doubt refers.

Why did we part in the very beginning?

I am now keeping your soul in a little Japanese box on my writing table. In it are all your letters—a ring set with a number of small rings (one is missing)—your bridal crown and veil—the gold pen . . . Let me write more beautiful things with it, beloved . . . And also two little bags of lavender, one red and one green, tied together with an indissoluble knot, from Denmark (1901).

The most beautiful of the letters are from 1904 (when we had parted). I am reading one, in which you reply to my petition for divorce with a cry of despair, and of crushed love! I read it as an outburst of woe to heaven, and I cry out from pain!

My bride of seven years ago . . . and now someone else's— and yet not!

Can you break this bond? Can you? I can not!

P.S. I "intend" to write a book on the Art of Acting. If I do, will you let me have the lovely portraits of yourself from Johannes *promptly*, then I shall lend you some beautiful reproductions of modern art that have to do with the theatre?

After fourteen days of negotiations with Ranft concerning your *Swanwhite*, he left yesterday without any answer. Unless he accepts the play, there is nothing we can do.

Would you want me to lose this favorable opportunity and do you wish me to wait for you! You know that I am used to waiting! But you—you have so many other things, and I have so little! And there is a prospect that I may have *Swanwhite* played at the Royal Theatre. That, however, is only a prospect! Falck will always give it—Ranft knows that—and with a little child seventeen years old who resembles you, can smile like you, but is of a melancholy turn of mind. She is cultivated, of good family. Will you not, if need be, adopt her as your pupil, your spiritual child, since you do not wish to have any earthly ones? Then you will still be acting, but through her.

I cannot understand why you will not let your talent give birth to new talent in others, and why you dislike the idea of giving birth to offsprings of your rare, strong soul. The bourgeoisie bring into the world ordinary children, but to spark a spirit in human souls—that is something only God's children can do.

I sometimes wonder whether any little spirit beings have been born out of our superhuman marriage. It seems to me that something must have been created out of such a union, in which forces of soul of unexampled stamina meet and melt into one.

Sometimes I think that you will have yet another child with me, although I do not know how. And it would be born in love and grow into a giant on earth—mighty in his humble position, through words and deeds. In my imagination I feel as if some little soul were waiting for us to be its parents, and I feel as if I had seen its little face against the white sheet in the moonlight. . . .

I take this opportunity to tell you something so that you will not be frightened if anything should happen. I have read in "a book" that there have been cases of simulated pregnancy, with all the symptoms, yet not real pregnancy! I wonder whether we can expect such a happening? I have also read—though I still doubt it—that true immaculate conception can take place; in brief, telepathically! What would we say . . . what would the world say?

But in any case I would know it through my feelings; for I have your soul bodily within me. I feel every mood and emotion of yours: When you are happy, when you are being pained (then I feel a spike in my heart) . . . and when He is discontent with me, I get a feeling as if something were bursting inside me.

11 April, 1908.

Must write you still another word!

Yesterday, when I was writing to Castegren, I did so with my heart sadly broken, after having reread our letters and after weeping for two days. But I was not convinced of my honesty of heart and I prayed to God not to let me become a hypocrite —which one is likely to become at such a time. And then I fell asleep. . . .

This morning I feel like a wretch and almost a hypocrite, although my feelings [as I expressed them] in my letter to C - n [Castegren] were genuine. I am convinced that he would die, if he were to be the victim of a short circuit in our alternate currents—I know that from experience—and I believe he has seen us in the dark of night. This is woeful, and the very worst I have ever experienced, this is . . . and it was the only thing I feared when you became engaged. Yes—I feel it whenever he caresses you; and I struggle against committing suicide.

This is what you have been toying with, child, in childish folly!

Fortunately I have never seen him, but yesterday I saw a photograph [of him]! He resembled me; but his self was dead—and he had become so much like me that he seemed like an offshoot of my soul—from playing my plays and from associating with you! He was I—I in the large portrait of myself—I in all my youthfulness. I did not begrudge you that youthful appearance of his in preference to my older appearance. But he himself was dead!

What can this be? Can souls bear offshoots? Yes—I have read so in a profound book.

But why do you go in for such incendiarism, dear child?

One thing I know: I shall never survive your wedding night—not from envy but only because I imagine what the future holds. . . .

Very well—then I shall celebrate my blood wedding! God will grant me that after all that I have suffered! And I shall be allowed to go, before I—before my immortal soul—has been sullied! It does no good that I tell myself: why should he touch my woman?—She was not mine in the usual sense, and he was right, but she was my creation nevertheless; and in her there was something of me that he now touches . . . that is why I shall depart. . . .

Why don't you let go of me? What do you want with my old person? Take my soul, if you so wish, but let me go. . . .

This will end unhappily. . . .

I cannot fathom that you allow yourself to be thrust about

helplessly by events! That it has never occurred to you—as it has to me—to seek the only Anchor that holds firmly, securely! I have just dispatched the letter to C - n [Castegren]! But it is not from the heart, as it was yesterday! May God help us all!

There can be no solution except by my going far, far away, so that I won't hear anything of your marriage. For if I should remain, it would be impossible for me to keep in touch with you through our child. Lillan is partial to you, and she would talk also! In a word, I shall never be able to see her again!

Do not stand in my way! And do not lead me into sin!

Before the marriage he must resign himself to our corresponding. We have to disentangle the old and make arrangements as to the child! Tell him that frankly!

One of us will die from this! I shall gladly sacrifice myself! It is the only thing [to do]. And then there will be no one to blame . . . no one! I absolve you!

You know that he was at death's door two years ago. Did he die then—and was he given a new soul through you, with whom he has been in love ever since you met in Finland? Has his character changed with his illness? What brought on his illness? You? Or I? Perhaps! You—who have been playing with dolls, so. . . .

Haven't you noticed that all who attempted to take you away from me, were stricken, died, lost wife and children? I took no hand in the matter, hardly dared nurture a desire to hurt them. . . . I knew how dangerous it was!

Therefore I am afraid to disturb you, for then I shall suffer pain.

And so: Let go of me!

You must not have more than one [husband]. Two would be murderous, criminal!

12 April, 1908.
Palm Sunday morning.

After your dear letter this morning—but only after you had confessed—I believe I have the right to say this. The heart is unreliable, adulterated, and I am partial in the matter. I cannot place any trust in noble motives when giving you advice—the worst thing one can do when it concerns an engaged couple. (You were given advice, too, once, and so was I, but it didn't do any good!)

What have you done, poor Harriet? Little Heart, what have you done?

There is only One who can help—God Almighty, The Creator! Now you are sinking, Harriet!

And our child, Lillan! . . . Anne-Marie! Oh God in Heaven, help us!

Now remains only one question, the same one I put to you when I asked for your hand: Will you have a little child by me? And you answered with a smile—as Anne-Marie sometimes smiles.

I knew all this last Saturday night, but I was too lacking in conceit to believe it.

Will you have a little child by me, Harriet?

[*April, 1908.*]

I accepted your engagement with quiet resignation. I gave you as an engagement gift my most beautiful possession: I was unselfish. But you wanted me to suffer; and you grew angry with me because I did not suffer.

Do Not Play With Love * are words you have seen on every street corner for the past month.

The banns you are publishing are hollow formalities without binding power, and they have not the slightest effect on my feelings, you know that! Don't speak about them . . . no one puts any faith in them—for all your engagement secrets are in plain sight!

But if you should marry, out of wickedness and vindictiveness, then I shall be free! And you, poor child, will be imprisoned! Wake up—live life—and do nothing but act in the theatre!

When I pleaded with you to let me be crucified for your

* A light comedy being given at one of the Stockholm theatres at that time.

sake, offered you in earnest the greatest sacrifice a man can make, then you answered by playing hide-and-seek!

Can the temple of happiness be built on sand? No! From now on I can only believe in a reunion on the other side . . . Have you ever seen a man showing devotion in every fibre, as he opens up his arms and offers his brow to her whom he has found once more!

There is no assurance that they who have found happiness *in der Ferne* will find it in *der Nähe!*

But no matter what: Give me faith, give me beautiful thoughts, give me the golden pen! Else it will be so hard to live! ! !

14 April, 1908.

What happened last night between half past ten and half past eleven, I do not know, but *you two* almost broke my heart! Your little heart was beating so hard in *my* breast that I had to lay my hand over it . . . and, lo, then it was silent and ceased to beat—and I thought you had died. . . .

But then, as I lay in the faithful blue bed that never had thought of any other woman but you, I had you lying on my arm, I could see your little face, feel your breath . . . and I took your little hand in the dark, kissed it and whispered, as I used to: Good night, dearest, beloved wife!

Is it this that Beethoven called Die ferne Geliebte? It is in truth . . . I was too childish not to understand it until you came along. . . .

What is this? A higher life on a higher plane, which only we *Götterkinder* can live! And to this life you would consecrate an earthworm and introduce him into it! No, Agnes, Daughter of Indra, no! Let no profaning influence enter there—let that remain outside the temple!

At first I recoiled as from a crime! I will not be a hypocrite, I cried out to God. And I prayed that He would smite me as a sign that I was in disfavor with Him. But He did not strike me . . . He let the moon shine into my room, and at midnight He lay my lovely little wife upon my arm!

It is granted—I may do it! But notice well, only in the soft darkness of the night that transforms the mystery into innocence!

During the day, in the light of day, it becomes a sin! And then there is a pounding in all the walls. . . .

I think I know that your engagement was stillborn—and is dead! I think I know why, and also why you took him out of spite!

Not long ago I saved a burning woman . . . If I should now have saved you, then I am your good Ariel, your servant for life, unto death, and forever after!

But what will happen now?

You see, my child, the purest love was the strongest . . . is and will be!

17 April, 1908.

Yesterday morning, Tuesday, I woke up with the impression that I had just married again, and I asked you to speak one word—the word you know . . . that others will volunteer, but which I care to hear only from your lips.

I caused you no harm yesterday, neither by word nor thought, not even by a glance!

In the evening your answer came. . . .

You sent your child with the Slave's bracelet! At that moment the child ceased to be mine . . . I relinquished it . . . relinquish it now . . . I no longer wish to see her, in order to spare her little soul from your wickedness—you, the wickedest of all created beings!

You have now sunk so low that only One—The Almighty—can raise you up from the abyss. . . .

I did not cry yesterday—I turned into stone!

You black Swanwhite! You took with you all my good thoughts when you left!

Now take all the rest as well—everything! Take the child, too! And leave me!

But you sought me out at sunrise—and you found not my better self but my evil self at home . . . And the evil is what you love, or hate—whatever it may be called—but my soul alone can give you joy! And that you shall never again possess! . . .

Now the child is his—from this moment . . . The Earl's daughter becomes the Slave's—and her mother, too!

Oh woe!

And I who thought so beautifully of you—who believed so deeply in you . . . who cherished our secret so faithfully, even in my pride—cherished it to the point that I was afraid to speak your name—and dared not show in public with even a look or expression how happy and how rewarded I felt!

And during these fourteen days I have written so beautifully, speaking with you in my heart . . . If you ever should glance in that book and happen to read 36 pages, you will recognize them, and you will ask: Where did he obtain that?

[18 April, 1908.]

After a long Good Friday—which you will remember—when everything was a huge, sad mockery, the evening set in . . . Then my spirit calmed down, someone whispered in my ear: The innocent bracelet was a worthless plaything which you did not wish to take away from the child, and it was no treasure. Then I stood there, crushed again, yet I hardly could wish to have undone the trial we had gone through, for it was a necessity—at least it served a purpose.

Am I right [in my surmise]?

Yet—forgive—I sent you a thousand [crowns], and shall do so again, even if that was not what happened, but rather—as I imagined—if it were a demon who had maligned me.

I—who never could be anything but faithful to you in my heart—even if not always in speech!

My only question, which you may have misunderstood, is this: Are you free? That is the crucial question for me—for I will not live in crime! Why do you not answer? I shall, of course, keep your answer in confidence!

Do not let Anne-Marie come here until that question is answered! The little creature talks, and her prattle is mysterious, sometimes deadly!

Your *Easter* has been done! I have thanked you before, but

now thank you again, and again! The first time you read it, your beautiful little soul touched my lips—for the first time ... and *your soul*—but *only* your soul—is so lovely. ...

Last night you sought me like fire and roses, roses at my lips. Every morning the sun rises, I feel an unquenchable desire to give you something! But I am so heavy-handed, my gifts always so ineffectual, they do harm though intended to do good. ...

Whisper a wish to me: great or small! Preferably great! I wish to sacrifice, to do without something that I value in order to give you something in return for the happiness you bestow upon me by loving me—the happiness that only love of soul can give! There—you see!

But first and last: Answer—are you free? This need not bring other consequences than those you desire! Whatever you wish —as you wish!

Lastly, once more: Thank you for your *Easter* and your Easter-girl—which was yours:

It has given people joy—a joy of the right kind!

. . . . . .

When you had read your *Easter* for the first time, you came [to me] asking God to bless me! Now He has heard your prayer!

14 May, 1908.
[The date of the postmark.]

You are beginning to believe in happiness! So am I during these wonderful six weeks ... but your last two letters have robbed me of my faith.

Write me again!

[Written in pencil on the outside of the envelope:]
A lire sans peur!

(Ohne Vorsicht!)
[*May, 1908.*]

Thrice I have written and burned up these words from the bottom of my heart:

TO HARRIET BOSSE

Will you be my lawful wedded wife,
Before God, the law, and the world,
In weal and woe,
In faithful love,
Forever and ever?

Shall this be burned also?
Yes—or no?
But you must be free to enter into marriage, so that you can receive a blessed, welcome child in your lap and be in my embrace—which has never been open to any other woman than you since I first saw you, not even in thought!

Whenever you speak or write to me, remember that you do so to a man who neither can nor would dare to speak one word that is not the truth! Isn't it heartening to be able to rely on one lone human being? That is the very one you must not deceive or play with! That would be a sin!

[On a visiting card]

[*May*, 1908.]

To let!
(Immediately.)
Karlavägen 40, 3 (three) flights up.
Four rooms and kitchen, etc.
The rent need not be paid!*

[*May*, 1908.]

My dear, beloved little friend!
Your little heart is beating all day long!
You are unhappy, and it is as if you were calling to me!
Say but one word, one lone word! I shall answer in a friendly spirit! I shall help you out of all this! I will do anything for you, for both of you!
Say but one word!

August Sg.

* Strindberg offers Harriet Bosse in this note the apartment underneath his own at that address.

After the spring of 1908 I never saw Strindberg again. My daughter continued to visit him until a few months before his death. Since his illness had changed his appearance, he wished her to remember him as he used to look and asked that she visit him no more. He desired her memory of him to be only beautiful.

A week or so before he passed away, his housekeeper came to my home, carrying a huge travelling bag. In it lay only a letter to our daughter, Anne-Marie, and 1500 crowns in bills. Strindberg wrote to Anne-Marie saying he had recalled that he had presented me with a grand piano when we were married, and that he later had brought me sorrow by exchanging it for an upright piano.

"Perhaps Mamma now would like to buy a new grand piano for these 1500 crowns?" he said in the letter. It was as if he had had a desire to make up for a wrong he thought he had done.

After his death, a Japanese box was sent to me, containing all my letters to him and several little mementos, together with the little crown of myrtle, now withered, that I had worn as a bride on the day of our wedding.

NOTES

PAGE
13 NILS PERSONNE. Actor, theatre historian. Served as managing director of the Royal Theatre in Stockholm, 1898–1904.
"DOUBLE-TONGUED LANGUAGE." Refers to Harriet Bosse's having been born in Norway.
14 SKANSEN. A vast park in Stockholm, with ethnographic, zoological, and other exhibits showing peasant culture, fauna and nature indigenous to Sweden. Founded by Arthur Hazelius in 1891, it has an outdoor theatre where plays and musical events are presented during the summer months.
15 KRISTIANIA. The capital of Norway, now renamed Oslo.
The First Violin. A play by the Danish actor and playwright Gustaf Wied.
AUGUST PALME. Distinguished Swedish actor and stage director.
16 DAGMAR. Harriet Bosse's sister, married to Carl Möller, director general of the Building Commission of Stockholm at that time.
CARL LARSSON. Famous Swedish painter.
19 HANNAH JOËL. A Danish author who went through a crisis similar to Strindberg's Inferno crisis and wrote a book about it.
AMALIE SKRAM. A Danish-Norwegian author (1847–1905).
Le Trésor des Humbles. Written by Maurice Maeterlinck in 1897.
20 "I ask you to read the enclosed play" (*The Crown Bride*).
La Princesse Maleine. Maeterlinck's first play (1890).
AXEL BURÉN. Former chamberlain to Princess Eugenie of Sweden; managing director of the Royal Opera, 1892–1907.
TOR AULIN. Swedish violinist, composer and conductor.
21 THE ROYAL (DRAMATIC) THEATRE: The Royal Theatre.
22 RICHARD BERGH. Famous Swedish painter, who painted Strindberg's portrait in 1905.
24 *Le Prince de Byzance.* By Villiers de l'Isle Adam.
25 THE LADY IN *To Damascus.* The leading female rôle in the Strindberg drama, which Harriet Bosse created in Part I of the trilogy.
ÖSTERMALM (Ö.) 29, 46. Strindberg's telephone number.
20 HASSELBACKEN. A famous Stockholm restaurant with an outdoor garden, beautifully situated in the Djurgården district.

PAGE
27 ". . . the man you helped last Sunday." Harriet Bosse had asked Strindberg to aid a man in dire straits, and he had sent the man a sum of money. Enclosed in this letter was one of thanks from the man.
INEZ AND ALF. Harriet Bosse's elder sister, Fru Inez Ahlquist, and her nephew, with whom Harriet Bosse lived at that time.
28 *Inferno*. Strindberg's famous account of his mental crisis, which he wrote in 1897.
Swanwhite. A fantasy or fairy play written for Harriet Bosse. She never did act the title rôle as intended.
Easter. The play had its Swedish première at the Royal Theatre the following day, April 4, 1901. Its original première took place in March, 1901, at Das Schauspielhaus in Frankfurt am Main in Germany.
29 ELEONORA. The central female figure in *Easter*.
30 G. AF G. (GUSTAF AF GEIJERSTAM), 1859–1909. Popular Swedish author; publisher. He wrote many plays and novels.
FREDRIK NYCANDER (1867–1944). Actor, author and critic.
P. S. (PEHR STAAF). Journalist and playwright.
TOR H-G (TOR HEDBERG), 1862–1931. Author, playwright and critic. Managing director of the Royal Theatre, 1910–21; member of The Swedish Academy.
31 AXEL STRINDBERG. August Strindberg's eldest brother (1845–1927). Insurance executive; conductor of the Royal Theatre Orchestra.
GUSTEN STRIX. Harriet Bosse did not care for the name of August, and it was agreed that she would call him Gusten. Strix: Latin for owl.
33 SIMON OF CYRENE. See: St. Mark 15:21; St. Luke 23:26; St. Matthew 27:32.
34 GUSTAV ADOLF. In English frequently Gustavus Adolphus.
"I won't let go Your hand until You bless me". These words occur again in the final scene of Strindberg's last drama, *The Great Highway*, translated by Arvid Paulson and published by Liveright Publishing Corporation—The American-Scandinavian Foundation.
MASTER OLOF DAY. April 19 has been named for Olavus Petri, the Swedish religious reformer.
35 *Midsummer*. A serious comedy in six scenes by Strindberg.
36 JOSEPH PÉLADAN. His occult, mystical writings interested Strindberg greatly.
EMIL SCHERING. Strindberg's principal translator into German.
38 "The beautiful pangs of conscience" and the Mosel intoxication. Strindberg is quoting from *To Damascus*, I.
NINTH SYMPHONY. Beethoven's Ninth Symphony.

NOTES

PAGE
- 39 BELLMANSRO } Popular restaurants in Stockholm.
  DJURGARDSBRUNN
- 43 VILHELM K. HEROLD (1865–1937). Distinguished Danish opera singer; managing director of the Royal Opera in Copenhagen, 1922–24.
- 47 CARL G. LAURIN. Noted Swedish literary critic and author.
  KARL NORDSTRÖM. Well-known Swedish artist.
  CARL ELDH (1873–1954). Professor; distinguished Swedish sculptor who made several statues and busts of Strindberg.
- 48 ALEXANDER L. KIELLAND (1849–1906). Noted Norwegian author.
- 50 B. Strindberg's strange nature drove him to imagine many things. This often led to the estrangement of his friends.
- 51 ANNA HOFFMAN-UDDGREN. A well-known variety actress of that day.
  THE EASTER GIRL. Eleonora in *Easter*.
  LINDELIN. A female character in a novel of the famous Norwegian author Jonas Lie.
  BLASIEHOLMEN. A central district of Stockholm.
  EMERENTIA POLHEM. A leading character in Strindberg's historical drama *Charles XII*.
- 52 ". . . there will be no children." A reference to the harlot: she bears no children.
- 56 LOVISA. Maid in the Strindberg home.
  [4 September, 1901.] In his Occult Diary Strindberg made an annotation, dated September 4: "Wrote a letter 'To my child.' Received a friendly answer."—His daughter Anne-Marie was born on 25 March, 1902.
- 58 RICH. B. Richard Bergh.
  Engelbrekt. One of Strindberg's historical dramas.
- 59 VERNER VON HEIDENSTAM (1859–1940). Author. Once an intimate friend of Strindberg's; he was awarded the Nobel Prize for Literature in 1916.
  EMIL SJÖGREN (1853–1918). Distinguished Swedish composer.
- 60 HERCULES AND OMPHALE. Omphale was a queen of Lydia whom Hercules was forced to serve for three years. He had to wear female apparel and had to spin with the maids.
  ". . . the little one" Strindberg's and Harriet Bosse's as yet unborn child (Anne-Marie).
- 61 *The Sexton on Rån Island*. A short story, the title of which is: *The Romantic Sexton on Rån Island*. It is included in the volume: *Life in the Skerries* (1889).
  The Growing Castle. One of Strindberg's tentative titles for *A Dream Play*.
- 62 SALTSJÖBADEN. A popular bathing resort just outside Stockholm.

PAGE
63 (8 September, 1901.) The date of this letter has been inserted by Strindberg.
64 EMIL GRANDINSON. Author and stage director. Staged productions at the Royal Theatre, 1898–1911.
    Simoon. A one-act tragedy in which Strindberg shows the influence of Edgar Allan Poe.
    Kristina. Strindberg's historical drama about Queen Kristina of Sweden.
65 ÖRESUND. The sound separating Sweden and Denmark on which the ancient city of Elsinore, of Hamlet fame, is situated.
67 STRANDVÄGEN. A fashionable thoroughfare in Stockholm.
    (20 September, 1901.) The date has probably been inserted by Strindberg.
69 ANDERS FRYXELL (1795–1881). Famous Swedish historian.
    CLAS TEODOR ODHNER (1836–1904). Swedish historian.
    WALTER CRANE. An English painter of the Pre-Raphaelite school.
    KNUT MICHAELSON. He was active in the Swedish theatre and wrote a number of plays.
    King René's Daughter. A drama by the Danish author Henrik Hertz (1797–1870). Tschaikovsky's opera *Iolanthe* is based on this play.
70 ÖSTERMALM PENSION. A fashionable boarding house in Stockholm.
    ". . . at the Möllers'." Harriet Bosse's sister Dagmar and her husband, Carl Möller.
    AUGUST PALME. He created the rôle of *Charles XII.*
    AUGUST FALCK (1882–1938). Actor, stage director. He founded the Intimate Theatre, commonly known as the Strindberg Theatre, in Stockholm in 1907 and, with the aid of Strindberg, kept it alive until 1910. During that time he produced twenty-four of Strindberg's plays. He wrote a book about his association with Strindberg and the theatre.
76 ". . . the *hôtel garni* where Jörgensen's Eva stopped. . . ." Alludes undoubtedly to the character of Eva in a novel by the Danish author Johannes Jörgensen.
78 PUCK. Harriet Bosse made one of her first successes in that rôle in *A Midsummer Night's Dream.*
    HAGAR. Strindberg frequently identified himself with such historical characters as Hagar, Cartaphilus (Ahasuerus, The Wandering Jew), the Flying Dutchman, etc.
79 *The Man in the Corridor.* One of Strindberg's tentative titles for *A Dream Play.*
81 VILHELM PETERSON-BERGER. Distinguished Swedish composer and music critic.

NOTES 187

PAGE
82 SANDHAMN. A summer resort situated on an island in the outer skerries.
85 BERTHA. Strindberg's maid.
   The Hollander. A dramatic fragment by Strindberg, written in 1902.
86 LESSING THEATRE (BERLIN). The original première of *Swanwhite* did not take place until October 30, 1908. Fanny Falkner created the title rôle; the play was given by the Intimate (Strindberg) Theatre in Stockholm.
89 *Black Banners.* Written in 1904, this book, which ostracized Strindberg from many of his old friends, was not published until 1907. Although scathingly received by most critics, Dr. Fredrik Vetterlund of *Aftonbladet*, among others, praised the author's undeniable literary gift.
   ELLEN KEY (1849–1926). Noted Swedish sociologist who wrote many books on ethics, sex, and feminist problems.
92 MATHILDA JUNGSTEDT. A celebrated Swedish opera singer at the Royal Opera in Stockholm.
   MARIKA STIERNSTEDT. A noted Swedish author.
   OLGA RAPHAEL (MRS. LINDEN). An actress at the Royal Theatre, noted for her beauty.
94 WAHL, ANDERS DE. A celebrated Swedish actor.
   ASTRI TORSELL. A noted Swedish actress.
   Lucky Per's Journey. A fantasy by Strindberg, written in 1882.
   GRETA STRINDBERG. Actress; Strindberg's daughter of his marriage to Siri von Essen.
95 APPLAR ISLAND. An island in the Stockholm skerries.
   BLID ISLAND. Situated in the Stockholm skerries.
96 A *Venetian Comedy.* By Per Hallström, a member of The Swedish Academy.
99 ISOLA BELLA. A name Strindberg gave to the cottage he occupied at Furusund.
   SIGRID. Harriet Bosse's maid.
104 SISTER PHILP. Strindberg's sister Anna, married to Hugo Philp.
105 JAMES MILLAR. Strindberg's attorney.
   Das Theater. A well-known German theatrical publication.
   HOTEL ORFILA. Strindberg lived for a time at this hotel during his mental crisis, which reached its culmination between 1894 and 1897.
   MME. CHARLOTTE'S. Mme. Charlotte, depicted in *Crimes and Crimes* in the rôle of Mme. Cathérine, owned a restaurant and lodging house chiefly frequented by struggling artists and literary figures.
   TORE SVENNBERG. A distinguished Swedish actor who at a later period was the head of the Royal Theatre in Stockholm.

PAGE

LILLAN. Diminutive of *the little one* used as an affectionate name for Anne-Marie.

106 ANDRÉ ANTOINE. Founder and director of the famous Théâtre Libre in Paris (1887). He was the first one to present Strindberg on the French stage.

PIERRE LOTI. A pen name adopted by the French naval officer Louis Marie Julien Viaud (1850–1923), who became known for his impressionistic writings in exotic settings.

108 ELLEN. A maid.

115 SVEA. Strindberg's maid at that time.

117 ELISABETH STRINDBERG (1857–1904). Strindberg's sister, who suffered from mental aberrations. She was the prototype of Eleonora in *Easter*. Strindberg's mother bore the name of Eleonora, as did a younger sister, Eleonora Elisabeth, who died a year after her birth (1850–1851).

119 MÖLLE. Swedish seaside resort on The Sound, opposite the Danish coast.

HELSINGBORG. Ancient Swedish city on The Sound. It is situated directly opposite Elsinore in Denmark. It was in that city Strindberg finally found a publisher for his drama *The Father* (1887) and for *Comrades* (1888), when they were published by Hans Österling, newspaper editor and publisher.

LUND. Ancient Swedish city with a university, founded in 1668. Strindberg lived in this city from December, 1897, to the middle of 1899, except for a brief visit in Paris.

120 TÄCKHOLMEN. An island in the Stockholm archipelago.

122 THE SVENNBERGS. Tore Svennberg and his wife.

124 E-N. Ellen, the maid.

126 ROSA. Anne-Marie's name for her doll.

HENNING BERGER. Renowned Swedish novelist and playwright. His play, *The Deluge*, won international fame; it was presented on the New York stage in 1917 by Arthur Hopkins, who also directed a radio performance of it.

"My book . . ." This probably refers to *Historical Miniatures*, which was published in 1905. His *New Swedish Adventures* was written in 1905 and published in 1906.

GERTRUD EYSOLDT. A distinguished German actress who was a member of Max Reinhardt's famous acting ensemble and created a number of Strindberg rôles in Germany.

127 *Tasso. Torquato Tasso*, which Goethe first wrote in prose and later in verse.

GÖTA KÄLLARE. A popular restaurant and barroom in Gothenburg.

GUSTAF JANSON (1866–1913). A Swedish author.

NOTES

PAGE
131 GREAT MEYER. Strindberg no doubt had improvised a game with the aid of the encyclopedia.
VILHELM CARLHEIM-GYLLENSKÖLD. A Swedish scientist; one of Strindberg's intimate friends.
132 SARAH. One of the many maids Strindberg employed during this period of his life.
JAKOB WASSERMANN (1873–1934). A noted German-Jewish author.
134 JULIET. *Romeo and Juliet.*
135 VICTOR CASTEGREN. Director of the Grand Theatre in Gothenburg; later stage director at the Swedish Theatre in Stockholm.
136 UNCLE LARSSON. Carl Larsson, who painted one of the finest portraits of Strindberg.
ELIN. Strindberg's maid.
139 RICHARD VALLENTIN. A well-known German theatre owner and stage director.
Simoon. A one-act thriller, reminiscent of Edgar Allan Poe, in which Harriet Bosse had given an electrifying performance at the Royal Theatre in Stockholm in 1902.
140 FRIEDRICH HEBBEL (1813–1863). Author of *Herod and Marianne.*
142 STOCKSUND. Not far from Stockholm.
ALBERT RANFT (1858–1938). Noted Swedish theatre owner, producer and actor; managing director of the Royal Theatre, 1909–1910.
BETTY NANSEN. A distinguished Danish actress and theatre director, whose appearances in silent motion pictures won her international fame.
GUSTAF FREDRIKSON. A distinguished Swedish actor and theatre director.
. . . the King. Oscar II (1829–1907).
. . . the New Theatre. The newly erected Royal Theatre.
BARON CARL CARLSSON BONDE. An overseer of the Royal Theatre at that time.
146 ALBERT BONNIER. The publisher of Strindberg's collected works.
147 *The Confessions of a Fool. Le Plaidoyer d'un Fou,* which Strindberg wrote in French and in which he defamed his first wife, Siri von Essen.
ISADORA DUNCAN. Internationally known dancer.
ALBERT ENGSTRÖM (1869–1940). Professor, satirist, wit and philosopher, as well as a distinguished artist; member of the Swedish Academy. He wrote a book about Strindberg.
EDWARD GORDON CRAIG (1872–   ). A son of the celebrated Ellen Terry; actor, author, artist and stage producer.

PAGE
148 ARMAS JÄRNEFELT. Finnish composer and conductor.
     Sv. D. Svenska Dagbladet. The leading conservative newspaper of Sweden.
149 CARL DAVID AF WIRSÉN. Poet and critic. Served as permanent secretary of the Swedish Academy, which awards the Nobel Prize for Literature.
     . . . the governor-general's banquet. Nikolai Ivanovitch Bobrikov, the previous Russian governor-general of Finland, had been murdered in 1904 by a Finnish patriot.
150 RUBENSON. The reference may be to Albert R. Rubenson, composer and critic.
     VILHELM STENHAMMAR (1871–1927). Composer; conductor at the Royal Opera in Stockholm.
     CONNY WETZER. Finnish theatre producer.
     EBBA. One of Strindberg's maids.
152 HOLGER DRACHMAN (1846–1908). A well-known Danish painter who became known, primarily, as a poet.
153 HILDA BORGSTRÖM. Celebrated Swedish actress, noted for her tragic rôles.
154 Alone. One of Strindberg's many autobiographical novels, written in 1903.
     19°. Centigrade (Celsius).
156 FRU v.E. Siri von Essen, Strindberg's first wife. She died in Finland, where she was born, in 1912.
157 ARE. A mountain resort in western Sweden close to the Norwegian border.
158 SWEDEN-NORWAY. Until the preceding year (1905) Sweden and Norway had been united under one king.
159 Idun. A Swedish periodical noted for its literary and cultural contributions.
     DROTTNINGHOLM. A royal castle, situated near Stockholm.
     THE NATIONAL THEATRE. The Royal Theatre.
     GRIPSHOLM. An ancient castle, the most beautiful and historic in Sweden, abounding in memories of the past. Situated not far from Stockholm.
     AUGUST LINDBERG. A famous Swedish actor.
     "the King wept . . ." Oscar II, who died the following year.
161 MY HANDS ARE BLEEDING. Strindberg suffered from psoriasis; also he had injured his hands during chemical experiments.
162 ÅNGERMANLAND; JÄMTLAND. Provinces in Sweden.
166 The Tale of Knight Huon. A thirteenth-century French legend of knighthood.
181 KARLAVÄGEN 40. Strindberg offers Harriet Bosse in this note the apartment underneath his at that address.

INDEX

A

Agnes (A Dream Play), 61, 177
Alf, 99, 110, 116–117
Alma, 74
Alone (novel), 154
Anne-Marie (Strindberg), 17, 46, 80, 81, 87, 89, 91, 94, 95, 100–103, 105, 107, 109, 110–112, 115–118, 124, 126–128, 131–134, 136–138, 142–143, 149–150, 152–154, 157, 159, 161–162, 165, 168, 175–176, 179, 181

B

Baltic, The, 151
Balzac, Honoré de, 19, 24, 47, 154–155
Banérgatan, 14, 16, 21, 31, 84, 135, 154
Banville, Théodore de, 13
Beethoven, 81, 92, 103, 104, 105, 133, 142
Bellmansro, 38
Berger, Henning, 126, 142, 147–150
Bergh, Richard, 22, 47, 52, 58, 92, 133, 136–138, 150
Berlin, 46, 48, 57, 60, 86, 144
Bertha, 85
Beyond (Joël), 19
Bianca, 70
Birger Jarlsgatan, 69
Björnson, Björnstjerne, 48, 89
Black Banners, 89
Blasieholmen, 51
Blid Island, 95, 128, 162
Bobrikov, Nikolai Ivanovitch, 149
Bonde, Baron Carl Carlsson, 142
Bosse, Harriet, Letters from, 48, 49, 55–57, 63–64, 67–68, 70–74

Borgström, Hilda, 153
Buddha, 130
Burén, Chamberlain Axel, 20

C

Capella (the little goat), 164
Carlheim-Gyllensköld, Vilhelm, 92, 131, 133, 151
Castegren, 134, 137, 138, 166, 167, 173–175
Charles XII, 46, 64, 67, 69, 70
Charlotte, Mme. (Mme. Cathérine) in Crimes and Crimes, 105
Chrysaëtos, 41, 45, 84, 86, 166
Cologne, 128
Confessions of a Fool, The, 147
Corot, 47
Craig, Gordon, 147, 148, 150
Crane, Walter, 69
Crimes and Crimes, 14, 105
Crown Bride, The, 19, 20, 21, 22, 25, 30, 31, 137, 143, 148, 154–156
Cymbeline, 152

D

Dagmar (Möller), 16
Dance of Death, The, 18, 20, 22, 127, 129, 154
Danube, The, 123, 124
Daughter of Indra (A Dream Play), 143, 177
Desert Tale, A, 70
Deutsches Theater (Berlin), 126
Deutsches Volkstheater (Vienna), 139
Didring, Ernst, 13
Djurgården, 86, 90, 110, 149, 168
Djurgårdsbrunn, 38
Drachmann, Holger, 152

Dream Play, A, 40, 41, 61, 79 (See also: *The Growing Castle* and *The Man in the Corridor*)
Drottningholm, 159, 168
Duncan, Isadora, 147, 148, 150, 157
Duse, Eleonora, 144

E

Easter, 18, 19, 22, 23, 24, 26, 28, 29, 31, 34, 45, 51, 117, 121, 128, 132, 134, 143, 153, 155, 168, 179, 180
Ebba, 118, 126, 134, 150
Eldh, Carl, 47, 133, 142, 149
Eleonora (*Easter*), 19, 23, 26, 29, 34, 45, 117, 132, 143, 153, 168, 179, 180
Elin, 136, 137, 141
Ellen, 108, 110, 111, 121, 124
Elsinore, 45
Emerentia Polhem (*Charles XII*), 46, 64, 67, 69
Emerson, Ralph Waldo, 48, 105, 106
Engelbrekt, 58, 62
Engström, Albert, 147, 150
Essen, Siri von, 147, 156

F

Face of Death, The, 14
Fahlström's Theatre, 14
Fairy Tales, 107
Falck, August, 70, 172
Figaro, Le, 94
First Violin, The, 15, 22
Formula (for making gold), 160
Fredrikson, Gustaf, 142
Fröding, Hugo, 110, 111, 134
Frölich, 158
Furusund, 99, 103, 104, 106, 107, 119, 123, 151, 157
Fryxell, Anders, 69

G

Geijerstam, Gustaf af, 30
Goethe, 127
Gorki, Maxim, 48
Gothenburg, 127, 128, 132, 136, 139, 144
Grandinson, Emil, 64, 67
Grand Theatre, The (Gothenburg), 124

Greta (Strindberg), 94, 104, 149, 150, 162
Grev Magnigatan, 29, 51
Great Meyer, 131
Grieg, Edvard, 59, 81
Gripsholm (Castle), 159
Growing Castle, The (A *Dream Play*), 61
Gringoire, 13
Grunewald (Germany), 46, 143, 164
Gustav Adolf, 34, 36
Gustav Adolf Church, 34
Gustav Vasa, 13
Gustav III, 139
Gyllensköld (Carlheim-), Vilhelm, 92, 131, 133, 151
Gärdet, 41
Göta Källare (Gothenburg), 127

H

Hagar, 78
Hasselbacken, 25
Hauptmann, Gerhart, 145
Hebbeltheater, Das. (Theater an der Königgrätzerstrasse, Berlin), 140
Hedberg, Tor, 30, 94, 149
Hedvig (*The Wild Duck*), 132
Heidenstam, Verner von, 59
Heine, Heinrich, 122, 133
Helsingborg, 119
Helsingfors (Helsinki), 107, 109, 112, 144, 146, 148
Hercules-Omphale, 60
Herod and Marianne, 140
Herold, 43
Hervor (Lindström), 127, 133
History of Sweden, The, 124, 126
Hoffman, Anna, 51
Hollander, The, 86, 87
Hornbaek (Denmark), 43, 45, 50, 119, 121, 157, 158
Hôtel Rydberg, 38, 168

I

Ibsen, Henrik, 145, 159
Idun, 159
Indra's Daughter (A *Dream Play*), 41
Inferno, 28, 68, 79
Inez, 27, 52, 99, 108, 110, 139, 141, 142, 150, 154
Iolanthe, 79

INDEX

J
Janson, Gustaf, 127, 158
Joel, Hannah, 19, 24
Juliet (Romeo and Juliet), 94, 134
Jungfrugatan, 31
Jungstedt, Mathilda, 92
Jämtland, 161
Järnefelt, 148
Jörgensen's Eva, 76

K
Karin, 162
Karlavägen, 40, 41, 56, 74, 76, 80, 81, 103, 108, 122, 141, 142, 143, 152, 157, 181
Kersti (*The Crown Bride*), 20, 21, 31
Key, Ellen, 89, 90
Kielland, Alexander, 48
King Lear, 106
King René's Daughter, 69, 70
Kipling, Rudyard, 24, 48
Kommendörsgatan, 73
Kristiania (Oslo), 14
Kristina, 65, 66–70, 72, 73, 76, 77, 79, 138, 168
Königgrätzerstrasse, Das Theater an der, 140

L
Lake Mälar, 81
Lady, The (*To Damascus*), 23, 25, 31
Larsson, Carl, 16, 133, 136
Laurin, Carl G., 47
Leipzig, 128
Lessing Theatre (Berlin), 86
Liding Isle Bridge, 110, 151
Lillan. See: Anne-Marie Strindberg
Lindelin, 51
Linden, Mrs. (Olga Raphael), 93
Lindberg, August, 159
Lindström, Captain, 127
Lisa (*Lucky Per's Journey*), 94
Loti, Pierre, 106
Lovisa, 55, 56, 58, 73, 74, 79
Lucky Per's Journey, 94
Lund, 119
Luxembourg Gardens, 105

M
Maeterlinck, Maurice, 19, 20, 24, 47, 48, 105, 106, 124, 136, 145
Man in the Corridor, The (*A Dream Play*), 79
Mary Stuart, 65
Master Olof Day, 34
Marianne (*Herod and Marianne*), 140
Midsummer, 35
Midsummer Night's Dream, A, 15, 46
Millar, James, 105, 110
Millet, 47
Miss Julie, 126, 147
Moloch, 132
Multrå, 161
Museum of the North, 17
Mölle, 119, 159
Möller, Dagmar, 16, 70

N
Nakkehoved, 65
National Museum (Stockholm), 47, 149
National Theatre, The (Royal Theatre), 159
New (Royal) Theatre, The, 142, 164
New Swedish Adventures, 149
Niece (Swedenborg), 19
Ninth Symphony, 38
Nordström, Karl, 47, 92, 133
North Blasieholm Harbor, 22
Novalis, 105
Nybroviken, 22
Nycander, Fredrik, 30

O
Odhner, 69
Old Heidelberg, 94, 106
Olympia, 73, 147
Orfila, Hôtel (Paris), 105

P
P.S. (Pehr Staaf), 30
Palme, August, 15, 23, 52, 70
Paris, 97, 103
Péladan, 36
Pelléas and Melisande, 124, 131, 132, 134, 135, 136, 138
Personne, Nils, 13, 21, 30, 79

INDEX

Peterson-Berger, Vilhelm, 81
Philipot, 119
Pickwick (Papers), 69
Play on Words and Art in Miniature, 107
Poet's Reward, The, 86
Politiken, 46
Prince de Byzance, Le, 24
Princesse de Maleine, La, 24
Puck, 15, 78, 145

R

Ranft, Albert, 79, 137–139, 140, 142, 145, 151, 152, 154–156, 166, 172
Raphael, Olga (Mrs. Linden), 93
Reinhardt, Max, 126, 142, 143, 164
Revsund, 161
Romeo and Juliet, 134
Rosendal, 110
Royal Theatre, The, 46, 79, 80, 172
Rubenson, 149
Russia, 139
Rävsnäs, 81, 82, 84, 85, 86, 95, 157

S

Saltsjöbaden, 62, 96–97
Sandhamn, 82
Sarah, 126, 132
Scapegoat, The, 157
Schering, Emil, 36, 46, 73, 105, 121, 129, 131, 139, 142, 145, 150, 159, 164
Schubert, 81
Schumann, 81
Secret of the Tobacco Barn, The, 41
Seraphita (Balzac), 19, 24
Sexton on Rån Island, The, 61
Shakespeare, William, 152
Shaw, English composer, 150
Sibelius, Jean, 148, 164, 166, 168
Sirishoo Bay, 125, 129
Simoon, 65, 77, 139, 145
Skram, Amalie, 19
Sophocles, 145
Staaf, Pehr, 30
Sterner, Miss, 22
Stenhammar, Vilhelm, 150
Stiernstedt, Marika, 93
Stockholm, 164
Stocksund, 142, 152, 154
Stormclouds (*Wetterleuchten*), 164
Strandvägen, 67

Strindberg, Axel, 31, 103, 108, 133, 150
Strindberg, Elisabeth, 117
Svea, 115
Svensson, Miss, 22
Svennberg, Tore, 105, 122, 151
Sv.D. (Svenska Dagbladet), 148
Swanwhite, 28, 31, 36, 40, 51, 65, 66, 68, 69, 70, 77, 78, 86, 135, 143, 148, 154, 156, 164–169, 172
Swedenborg, Emanuel, 19
Swedish History, 124, 126
Swedish Theatre, The, 41, 62, 94, 109, 142, 151, 165
Switzerland, 132

T

Tale of Knight Huon, The, 166
Tales, 41
Taming of the Shrew, The, 153
Tammelin, Bertha, 13
To Damascus, 15, 17, 23, 25, 31, 32, 105, 139
Torquato Tasso, 127
Torsell, Astri, 94
Totten, 161
Trésor des Humbles, Le, 19, 48
Trinity Night, 41
Täckholmen, 120, 154

U

Uppsala, 149

V

Vallentin, 139, 143
Venetian Comedy, A, 96
Vesuvius, 154
Vienna, 132, 140, 145

W

Wahl, Anders de, 94
Wassermann, 132
Wetterleuchten (*Stormclouds*), 164
Wetzer, C., 150, 164
Wild Duck, The, 132, 145
Wilde, Oscar, 148
Wirsén, Carl David af, 149
Wyller, Anne-Marie (*See* Anne-Marie Strindberg)

Z

Zola, Émile, 48